BOOKS BY PROF. JOHN C. VAN DYKE

PALMA VECCHIO, Santa Barbara (detail). S. M. Formosa, Venice.

THE MEANING OF PICTURES

SIX LECTURES GIVEN FOR COLUMBIA UNI-
VERSITY AT THE METROPOLITAN
MUSEUM OF ART

BY

JOHN C. VAN DYKE

AUTHOR OF "ART FOR ART'S SAKE," "NATURE FOR
ITS OWN SAKE," ETC.

WITH ILLUSTRATIONS

NEW YORK
CHARLES SCRIBNER'S SONS
1920

TO

WILLIAM CRARY BROWNELL

PREFACE

Just how we should look at pictures, just how we should judge of them, is not for any one person to say. We all have our different ways of estimating art; and art is capable of being estimated in different ways. In these lectures I have endeavored to set forth the various points of view. The painter's conception has received perhaps the primary attention, but I have given the public's conception of the picture also. Nor do I mean to apologize for arguing both sides of the case. Art might be better understood, if there were less special pleading and theorizing about it. It is so largely dependent upon the individual make-up of the artist, that any precise theory about it must fall short of the mark. Instead of quarrelling over terms and trying to put the opposition in the wrong, it would be better frankly to examine the product in the light of the producer's intention and draw our conclusions from that. We should not always agree, but that is all the more reason for tolerance and liberality.

J. C. V. D.

Rutgers College,
    November, 1902.

CONTENTS

CONTENTS

LIST OF ILLUSTRATIONS

THE MEANING OF PICTURES

THE MEANING OF PICTURES

CHAPTER I

TRUTH IN PAINTING

THOSE people who go out into the highways of art crying, Haro! Haro! in the name of realism, would certainly gain their cause could numbers give them a verdict. They have always been in evidence; they have always made themselves heard. There never was a time when the mob was not hungry for realities, when artists were not harping upon "truth to nature," when critics were not concerned about "the realistic tendencies of the age." The interest in things as things and the art that hinges upon facts as facts were from the beginning. For did not Apelles paint horses so realistically that other horses neighed at the sight of the picture? And did not Zeuxis deceive the birds with his painted grapes, and was not he himself deceived in turn by the painted curtain of Parrhasios? Admitting the stories to be greatly exaggerated, does not their very existence prove the liking for the realistic motive?

Indeed, the Greeks were accounted very good realists in the days of their late power. The Pergamon frieze, the "Samothracian Victory," the "Dying Gaul" give the proof. And in earlier times they modelled and chiselled the Parthenon marbles so true to life that William Hazlitt based a theory of art upon them, maintaining that the aim of art was the imitation of nature and the finest art was simply the imitation of the finest nature. It was the realistic Roman marbles, founded upon those of Greece, that gave the first breath of inspiration to the painters of Italy. The Renaissance nature-study that went hand in hand with the study of the Greek was largely to enable the painters to reveal the model more completely, to draw a leg or arm or face more exactly, to place figures in an atmospheric envelope, to reproduce a likeness of the landscape background. If we examine the works of Fra Filippo, Botticelli, or Mantegna, we shall find that there was more of the earthly in their painting than the mystic face of the Madonna or the religious pathos of saints would disclose. They were intent upon the reality before them and evidently for the reality's sake. They delighted in drawing a foot and placing it firmly upon the ground, in giving bulk, body, and weight to the figure, in painting flowers, leaves, and fruits with precision, in adjusting the exact relations of light-and-shade, in catching the right tone of color. It was all a close following of the model—a representation of nature itself or as near to it as they could attain.

But the Dutch painters of the seventeenth century were far more rigid sticklers for the fact than the Italians. Their work was essentially a portrait of Holland and its people, as Fromentin has said, wherein faithfulness to the model was a primary consideration. From Hals and Rembrandt down to Van Mieris and Schalken every Dutchman considered an object as a plastic fact—a something not to be juggled with, but to be rendered as truthfully as possible. Indeed, it was the Dutchmen who set the pace for all the moderns in what is called realism. It was the five days upon a lady's hand—a day to each finger—of Gerard Dou that suggested the ten days to a shoe-buckle of Meissonier. All the modern contingent of *genre* painters and students of still-life who paint things that "stand out" are but a growth from the Dutch. The tradition has been handed down unimpaired, losing none of its ancient positiveness, but rather gaining some latter-day exactness in the process of transmission.

For just now realism in art seems more of a *desideratum* than ever. And from the way the word "truth" is bandied about studio and gallery, one might think it the only thing worth having in artistic equipment. But we need not necessarily become either brow-beaten or bewildered by all this volume of talk about the real. For, bluntly stated, there is no such thing as absolute realism in art. The "real" is nature itself, and "truth" is merely the report of nature made by man. Some cattle and horses standing under a tree in a meadow are a reality, and your description or report of the scene, either in words, lines, or colors, would be the truth of the scene—that is, provided your description was accurate. Under no circumstances is the report made by producing the real things in evidence. It is practically impossible to do that in art. Any close attempt at doing it, or misleading one into thinking he sees reality, generally results in absurdity or repulsiveness. What, for instance, could be more hideous than the wax figure in the museum? Or what more dull than the modern battle-panorama where dummy-figures and painted figures mingle to make up the scene?

Art is far removed from such attempts. Instead of producing the real it merely implies or suggests the real by certain signs and symbols which we have agreed among ourselves to recognize as its equivalent. If, for instance, we attempt to bring to the mind of another the thought of water we do not get a glassful of it and place it upon the table to show what we mean. We simply say or write "water"—a word of five letters which bears no likeness or resemblance whatever to the original, yet brings the original to mind at once. This is the linguistic sign for water. The chemical sign for it, H_2O, is quite as arbitrary, but to the chemist it means water again. And only a little less arbitrary are the artistic signs for it. The old Egyptian conveyed his meaning by drawing a zigzag up or down the wall; Turner in England often made the few horizontal scratches of a lead pencil do duty for it; and in modern painting we have some blue paint touched with high lights to represent the same thing. None of these signs attempts to produce the original or has any other meaning than to suggest the original. They are signs which have meanings for us only because we agree to understand their meanings beforehand.

Now this agreement to understand the sign is what might be called the recognition of the convention. All art is in a measure conventional, arbitrary—unreal if you please. Everyone knows that Hamlet in real life would not talk blank verse with his latest breath. The drama (and all poetry for that matter) is an absurdity if you insist upon asking: Is it natural? It is not natural; it is very artificial. And unless you accept the artificial as symbolizing the natural, unless you recognize the convention of metre and rhyme, you are not in a position to appreciate verse. The name of those who " do not care for poetry " is legion, because they have not the proper angle of vision, because they are out of focus. And this is

equally true of music. Tristan and Isolde singing
their loves at each other is sheer insanity from a realistic standpoint. Everyone knows that love in real
life may do a good deal of sighing and sobbing, but it
does not burst forth into song. The opera is a most
palpable convention, and the flow of music, which
so beautifully suggests the depths of passion and the
heights of romance, is but an arbitrary symbol of reality. Recognize this and you have taken the first
step toward the understanding of art ; fail to recognize it and art must always be a closed book to you.
You will not perceive the artist's intention.

As a matter of fact we all do accept the convention
in one form or another. If a child standing at the
blackboard should draw a horse with four chalk-
lined legs and a chalk-lined body and head we should
have no trouble in making it out as a horse. And
should we know it as a horse because of its truth to
nature ? Is a horse flat, hairless, colorless, shadow-
less ? And has he a chalk line about him ? Not at
all. The representation is but a sign or symbol which
we have agreed to recognize as a horse. It is a
child's representation, and it differs from a painter's
representation of the same animal largely in the
matter of trained skill and imaginative conception.
The fine portraits of Holbein—than which there is
nothing finer in painting—have that same rim about
them (Plate 1). We call it Holbein's " clear outline,"

but it is substantially the same thing. And the etched landscapes of Rembrandt—what could you have more arbitrary? Merely a few lines drawn with a swift hand, a few scratches in a copper plate to represent sunlight, and some cross-hatchings to represent shadow; but how quickly we recognize their meanings! If you will look closely at the wood engravings of Timothy Cole you will see the modelling of the faces brought out sometimes by long, waving, diagonal lines, sometimes by dots and sometimes by checks and squares. Again could anything be more conventional? But we have no trouble in making out the artist's intention. We accept the convention from the start.

So it is that we do not necessarily grasp the intention by the fulness or elaborateness of the sign. The painter, from long experience, from being more expert of hand, is perhaps better able to exploit the sign than is the child; but we do not fail in understanding the meaning of the childish outline. There is a difference in sign making, to be sure, and that may make a great difference in art; but there is little or no difference in the intention—the meaning of the sign. The flat figures upon the Greek vases are not quite like the outlined figures of Raphael and Ingres, and still less like the figures of Manet; but they are all signs nevertheless. Manet used the patch of color instead of the rim or outline, which is supposed to be a very fetching piece of realism ; but none of the representations is to be mistaken for reality. The real is one thing ; the sign or symbol for it, quite another thing.

What then is realism in art—this drawing of eyes that follow you about the room, lips that seem parted as if to speak, and hands that you could shake ? What is this painting of pots and pans to be picked up, and cows that walk out of the canvas ? Can we not define it as merely the adding-to, the rounding, the perfecting of the sign ? Is it anything more than the telling of all the truths, both great and small, so that the veriest dunce in conventions shall not fail to recognize them ?

To revert to our former illustrations, perhaps Ingres's rigid outline contains less truth—less important truths—than Manet's color patch. Why ? Because the figure in full light really has no rim about it. It looks more like a patch of color relieved against other colors. The rim or outline is childish, primitive, and originally came, not from a direct study of the model but from studying the model's shadow or silhouette. People of childish intelligence, like the Egyptian fellaheen, for instance, understand it very readily because of its simplicity and its arbitrary utterance ; but the more complex sign that deals with sunshine rather than the flattened shadow contains the greater truth. Therefore as regards the

ANNO · DÑI · 1541 · · ETATIS · SVÆ · 2 8 ·

I.—HOLBEIN, Portrait of a Man. Belvedere, Vienna.

whole truth there is more of it in Manet's figure than in Ingres's. Additions to the sign, such as effects of light-and-shade, of color, of surface texture, of contour, may tell us more about the object and add to the sum of truth and the perfection of the sign ; and yet these may not change in any way the significance of the sign. The most elaborate human being that a Meissonier could paint would still be only the individual symbol of a man, and in that respect would not be different from the incised outline of Rameses the Great upon a Theban wall.

You will understand, of course, that there are painters who use the sign to convey a meaning—use it as one might words and sentences. Millet, in writing to a friend, said : " All art is a language and language is made to express thoughts." Of that I shall have something to say later ; but just now I wish to call your attention to the fact that the realist does not agree with Millet, that he is not concerned with ulterior meanings, that in fact he rather despises them. For realism, broadly speaking, means a pot for a pot's sake, or a cow for a cow's sake, which is to say a sign for a sign's sake. The Gerard Dous and the Meissoniers rather plume themselves upon being expert sign-makers. Their art usually goes no farther than excellent craftsmanship. They draw and paint skilfully, decoratively, telling everything about the model before them, from an eyelash to a boot-strap ;

and there they stop. They give forth an official report which may be true enough from their point of
view and yet contain not an idea worth the contemplating, not a thought worth the thinking. But that
does not in any way disturb the poise of the realist.
He is ready to answer you that "beauty is truth
and truth beauty"—an aphorism that sounds like
argument and yet is only assumption. But let us
look into the matter a little farther and ask : What
is the truth which they claim to have ? Is it the
vital truth or the only truth, and are there not vari-
eties, grades, and degrees of truth in painting as in
the other departments of art and life ? I have no
wish to deny that realism, so-called, makes up one
kind of art ; but let us push our inquiry farther
afield and find out if possible what is the basis of the
realistic picture.

"Truth," we have already affirmed, "is the report of nature made by man." We may cast out the
child's report about the horse because it is incomplete, immature. It is made up of all the errors of
the untrained hand and eye, and though it has a
certain personality about it, and gives us a child's
idea of a horse, yet it cannot be considered as an entirely truthful record. The report of the camera, if
it be true or false we do not know. Light flashes
and the horse's silhouette is instantly caught and
fixed upon the plate ; but I need not tell you that

light does not flash into the human eye, and the silhouette is not instantly fixed upon the human retina in the same way. Nor need I tell you that eyes vary more widely in the way they see than do cameras. Which then tells the truth? That the camera always records the same does not prove that it always records truly. It may always record falsely. At least the human eye sees differently from the camera, and the ultimate decision as to truth must be referred back to the eye. It may not be an infallible register, but it is the best we have. For all human knowledge must base itself upon human sensation.

The horse of the child being incomplete and that of the camera misleading, we return to the work of the painter and ask: What of the horse of Apelles? Can that stand as the final truth? The story of its deceiving other horses we may put aside as pure romance, but undoubtedly the picture was emphasized in its modelling—pushed hard in its high lights—to make the horse "stand out." Granted a truth of relief and perhaps a truth of surface, are these the only truths about the horse? And do they make the standard to which art and artists must bow? Not necessarily. We have had hundreds of painters since Apelles's time who have painted hundreds of horses, perhaps quite as true to nature as his, but never a one of them saw or painted a horse in just the way Apelles did.

And now we are confronted with the fact that if
there are many men of many minds in this world of
ours there are also many men with many eyes. No
two pairs of eyes see alike. Are we to infer then
that any one pair of eyes or any one race or its
school of painters sees truth and all the others see
only error? Is truth on one side of the Alps and
falsehood on the other? Titian in Italy made a different report of nature from Rembrandt in Holland
—which told the truth? Does truth abide exclusively in the Orient or the Occident? A landscape in
Japan by Hokousai, how very different from a Seine
landscape by Daubigny! But is either of them
false? And after all does not something of truth—I
do not say the whole of it—consist in the fidelity
with which the point of view is maintained? We
must cultivate liberality in this matter. For Creation ordained that there should be a Babel of eyes, all
seeing differently, and consequently there must be a
standard of truth peculiar to each individual.

Does "truth to nature" then mean to each man
what his eyes tell him and to each painter what the
sincerity of his make-up enables him to record? Yes,
certainly; but, mind you, it may be a very limited
truth, not necessarily an absolute truth, not a world-
embracing truth applicable to all classes and conditions of men. The child with his chalk-lined horse
may be maintaining his childish point of view with

II.—BENOZZO GOZZOLI, Adoration of Kings (detail). Riccardi Palace, Florence.

the utmost fidelity, but it is apparent from his drawing that he does not fully comprehend his subject,
does not see the object in its entirety. The horses
by Spinello Aretino, shown in his Campo Santo pictures at Pisa, are not very different from the child's
conception. They contain more truths without by
any means being exhaustive. They are still crude,
but true enough as regards the maintenance of the
point of view. The fine horses of Benozzo Gozzoli,
in the Riccardi palace fresco (Plate 2), are an improve-
ment upon those of Spinello without being complete,
and the Gattemalata horse of Donatello, the Colleoni
of Verrocchio, may make us enthusiastic about the
special truth of their pushing power, and again not
make a full report of the horse. Perhaps when we
reach the height of realism and come to a horse as
seen by Gérôme or Rosa Bonheur we are not so
pleased with it as with Benozzo's square-framed
beast; but that may be for a cause which we shall
discuss hereafter. The completeness of the truth,
the fulness of the report, may not be denied, however wearisome it may be as art.

Now we must add to this individuality, which
everyone possesses in measure and which must warp
the vision somewhat, a further influence or bias
which the individual takes from his race and his
country. I have already asked Pascal's question
about truth being on one side of the Alps and error

on the other side. Applied to the arts it is pertinent
to inquire: Is a Siena landscape by Pintoricchio
false because it does not look like a Vosges landscape
by Courbet? Not at all. They are both true—that
is, not only true to locality but true to that native
flavor which makes a pine-tree in Japanese art look
" Japanesey" and a pine-tree in Norwegian art look
Norwegian.* Moreover, each landscape is true in
exhibiting its time, its country, and its race. The
Pintoricchio shows the attenuated purist landscape of
the Tuscan country—the landscape admirably suited
to serve as a background for the sensitive, sentimental
saints he depicted. It speaks truly enough for a
portion of Italy during the Early Renaissance, that
portion which lies in the Tuscan country; but it
goes no farther. Giovanni Bellini at Venice was
Italian, too ; but he was at this very time producing
quite a different landscape—one that spoke for the
mountainous country lying to the north of Venice,
but not for Tuscany. The landscape by Courbet is

* " If we will take the trouble to look at the wood-cuts illustrative of some given celebrity as they appear in the illustrated
newspapers of various nations, we shall see that, though copied
very mechanically from the same photograph, Mr. Gladstone
becomes a Frenchman in France, a Spaniard in Spain, and,
though less visible to us, in the same way the Continental, the
Spaniard, or the Frenchman becomes English in the engraving
of an English magazine. Even in the handling of the tool
called the graver which cuts the wood there is, then, a nationality."—JOHN LA FARGE, in *International Monthly*, Nov., *1900*.

not so limited. It is nineteenth-century work and has the advantage cf the great advance made in landscape work since the Renaissance; and yet no one could fail to see that it was French, that it depicted a French country in a French way. With all its large truth of appearance it shows its localized Parisian point of view. To be sure Paris in Courbet's day was very cosmopolitan. His vision was broader, his grasp of truths greater than the sculptor who carved, in bas-relief, Sargon feasting with his wives; but nevertheless the local truths of France and of Assyria are each apparent in each.

Is every artist then biassed in his conception of truth by his race and age; and is every art significant of its environment? Certainly. Thus far in the world's history all art has been provincial—expressive at least of a nationality if not of a locality. The art of Holland in the sixteenth century never travelled beyond the dikes and dunes except in the case of a genius like Rembrandt. As a truth for universal application a roystering party by Jan Steen would go no farther to-day than a garden party under the cherry blossoms by Hiroshighe. Both are peculiarly provincial and belong in their own lands with their own peoples. Outside of their own countries they meet with appreciative understanding only from the artistic few. A century ago no one in the Anglo-Saxon or Teutonic world cared very much for Dutch art, and not fifty years ago Japanese art was regarded as little more than an interesting absurdity because of its unfamiliar perspective. Neither of them at this day has any world-wide reach. They have not travelled to us, but the cosmopolitan art-lover has gone out and discovered them. Transportation may eventually make us all cosmopolitan—make all art kin ; but it has not done so as yet.

Of course all painting is not so strictly local as the pictures of Jan Steen and Hiroshighe would suggest. A work of art, in subject and in method, appeals more strongly perhaps to its own people than to any other—an Osiris to an Egyptian, a Zeus to a Greek, and a Madonna to a Christian. But the carved Buddha, seated with crossed legs, open palms, and a vacant stare into space appeals only to a Buddhist. It will not travel elsewhere except as a curio. Nor will the Osiris or the Madonna go very far. But what of a Zeus ! what of a Hermes by Praxiteles ! what of the Greek ideal ! Have they not a universal quality about them—a grasp of universal truths—that carry them beyond the frontier lines of Hellas ? Think for a moment of the " Venus of Milo." Has it not something supremely true about it that a person of any nationality cannot choose but see ? And think for a moment of the " Ariadne " of Tintoretto. Again is there not something here that compels the admiration of the Asiatic as well as the European

III.—VAN DYCK, Cornelius van der Geest. National Gallery, London.

and the American? There is individual and local and racial truth in all these works, but there is also universal truth—truth applicable to all humanity. *stopped*

And now, if we stop to consider the great men in the arts, we shall invariably find that each one of them is marked by some quality of universal significance. There is something about them all that overleaps the provincial, the accidental, the small, and the trifling. They disregard in a measure the local truths and aim at the general truths—at things essentially true for all humanity. Our Shakespeares and Platos and St. Pauls survey the world from mountain tops. From these vantage points their perspective is far-reaching, their view of the world expansive. They see and grasp the essentials, the basic elements, the foundations of things. It is this, for one thing, that makes the art of Titian so superlatively great. What wonderful men and women people his pantheon! What types they are of manhood and womanhood! What embodiments of loftiness, dignity, and nobility! And are they not universally admired? No matter what a man's nationality, he cannot choose but be interested in "The Man with a Glove" or the "Charles V." at Madrid. There is something in them of that truth seen from mountain heights which every one will recognize as the nobler part of his little valley-world.

Just so with the art of Rembrandt. His type

is essentially of the Low Countries; his costumes, landscapes, light-and-shade, and methods are all localized in Holland. But a sadder painter you cannot find in all the reach of painting. His emotional nature had been wrung by trial and suffering and his sympathies were with the down-trodden and the grief-stricken. There never was a painter who painted so much of sorrow in the faces of his people as Rembrandt. The "Christ at Emmaus" is, in form and figure, only a poor emaciated Amsterdam Jew; but in emotional truth it is the one Christ of all painting. That face appeals to Christian, Mahometan, Jew, and infidel alike, not because of its divinity but because of its intense humanity. Should we bring up the names of the other great masters of painting we should find that each one of them is remarkable for some quality of universal significance—Michael Angelo for his great command of form, Rubens for his great splendor of effect, Velasquez for his sense of vitality in the physical presence (Plate 13), Raphael for his unity and his harmony.

The great men are remarkable for their breadth—the wide angle of their vision. They see, not differently from others, but they see more. Yet it is only a point of view, a limited outlook, and not by any means the total sum of truth. The report of nature made by man, which we have defined as "truth," is always a report of some sort whoever makes it. The difference between the great minds and the small ones consists in what is seen and reported. A Rousseau who sees and tells of the solidity of the earth, the volume of the forest, the great luminous expanse of the sky, does not think to tell everything that may be in the landscape. He sees the great truths, those truths that are of universal permanence in all landscape, and emphasizes them at the expense of the smaller details. A man of narrower vision would perhaps overlook the sky and earth, and fail to see the forest for the trees. He might centre all his interest in blades of grass, in dew-drops and spider-webs and opening buttercups—the infinitely little things in the landscape.

In portraiture men like Gerard Dou and Denner emphasize the small skin-facts of a man's face with such minute workmanship that you may study them with a magnifying-glass. You will never see anything like this in the portraits by Titian, Rembrandt, Velasquez, Van Dyck (Plates 3, 13, 18). They waste no time on small truths. They are intent upon giving the large physical presence, not the petty deformities of the epidermis.

Again in drawing a hand and arm you will observe that men like Gérôme give every curve and break of light along the arm, every accidental contortion of muscle, every wrinkle and twist of flesh ; but some-

how, when all these features are put down, the arm
fails to live, fails to move. It is a petrified arm.
For an opposite statement of truth look at the arm
of Millet's "Sower." There is nothing absolute
or minute about the drawing. The arm is gen-
eralized, summarized, synthetized as it were. The
wrinkles in it are not apparent, the covering of it is
vague, the hand is not articulated in the muscles or
even definite in the drawing of the fingers. In short
the whole arm and hand are cut down to a few ele-
mentary lines, so that they appear to the uninitiated
somewhat sketchy and peremptory. But looked at
for those qualities which Millet thought more important than surface texture, looked at for bulk,
mass, weight, motion—particularly motion—and
there is a larger view apparent. The arm and hand
certainly have motion and life. And these are precisely what Gérôme's arm and hand have not. Can
it not be claimed then that the truth of life and motion is a greater truth than the truth of momentary
rigidity ? Is it not a fact that Millet has seized upon
a general and universal truth characteristic of all arms
and hands—that is, the truth of life and movement—
whereas Gérôme has seized upon an accidental truth
of light-and-shade which may be something local and
peculiar to that one hand and arm ?

If one shows us a snap-photograph of breaking
waves, what do we see if not the highest and most

IV.—MILLET, The Gleaners, Louvre, Paris.

brittle wave the camera man could catch ? Does this give us a general or a particular truth of the sea ? Do waves stand rigidly in air, petrified from base to crest, as we see in the photograph, or do they roll and keep on rolling indefinitely and ceaseless-lessly ? Does not the very essence of truth about a wave lie in its restless heave and toss, its breaking and reforming, its eternal indefiniteness of form ? How many sea pictures have we seen with every wave in place—pounded into place like hammered steel— with every facet shining like a mirror, and not a pos-sibility of motion in anything ? Perhaps we have rather enjoyed them and fancied, in crossing the ocean, that the waves looked like that. Perhaps they did ; perhaps we were content to see only the small truths of the ocean ; but a study of the marines by Courbet, Manet, and Monet may convince us that there are larger truths of the ocean than those relat-ing to its mirror-like sparkles—larger truths in the ocean's depth, power, and its restless, ceaseless mo-tion. These painters have discarded small things on the surface of the water, as Frans Hals the small spots on a man's face, in order to give the sense of form back of it (Plate 22).

In the same way you will often find painters dis-carding the exact drawing of objects such as wood or cloth or stone or metal in order that they may give the weight, the elasticity, or the density of these objects. A feather or a leaf may be an epitome of floating, dancing lightness, but if you draw its complete anatomy and paint all its surface texture you will have something that is as heavy as wrought iron. It does not follow either, because Desgoffes gives us the sheen and flash of brasses, china, and satins, that he has told all or the most vital truths about those articles. Vollon may paint the same things in a fuller manner, showing us something of structural character which is just as important and just as true as surface appearance. Moreover, the broader method leaves something to implication and suggestion, where the other method buries under an accumulation of fact.

Please note the word "suggestion," for it is by suggestion that the greatest truths of art are brought home to us. The realist, whom we have been hastily considering, does not care for this method of approach. He is bent upon realization. He is analytical in his statement of each and every fact and makes a full report. All painters do this in some degree during the early stages of their career, but as they advance in years and experience there is a tendency to a broader treatment, a return to the simple line of the child, to the synthesis of a Millet, as shown in the arms, hands, and backs of the women in "The Gleaners" (Plate 4), to the implication and suggestion of a Corot, as shown in the sky of the "Biblis." Facts are summarized. A mere charcoal outline drawn by Degas gives us the reliefs, proportions, weight, and bulk of a human figure; a shadow with Giorgione or Rembrandt sums up the series of facts beneath it, and becomes suggestive by its very mystery and uncertainty; a blended blur of color by Whistler may bring to mind a heaving wave in mid-ocean better than all the drawn and tinted and "realized" waves of all the realists.

It is not the heaping of fact upon fact that flashes the truth upon us—at least not in art, though it may in logic or in law. Indeed, the accumulation of evidence often confuses. It is common studio experience that a sketch of a picture is frequently better than the picture itself. The attempt to "finish" (that is, to put in all the details and minutiæ) makes it dull and unsuggestive. The unfinished marbles of Michael Angelo, do they really suffer much by being unfinished? I have sometimes thought that the figure of "Day" in the Medici Chapel gained by its incompleteness—that it was better than the "Night" upon the opposite side of the tomb because the sculptor's intention is perfectly obvious and yet the spectator's imagination is not stifled. There, like a fallen god, he lies, half embedded in his matrix of stone with a suggestion of mighty power, never so strongly felt in any other marble in this world. The lack of finish, the mystery, the uncertainty, help on the imagination. One may fancy, as many have done, that the figure symbolizes the loss of Florentine freedom, and that the grand captive, with his massive brow and sunken eyes, half-rises wearily to view the morning light shining for him in vain. And again one may imagine he is a new Prometheus bound to the rock ; one of the Gigantes ; or perhaps a conquered Titan lying along the hills of Tartarus in the drear twilight, brooding in melancholy silence over the loss of Olympus. To whatever the mind may conjure up regarding the figure, the element of reserved strength will lend assistance. Cut the captive from his bed of stone and the strength falls short, lacking the foil of resistance ; finish the marble and an existent fact precludes the possibility of wide imagination.

The great English master of art, how well he knew what to leave out ! The lovers Lorenzo and Jessica are in the still, evening air, and with what consummate skill Shakespeare paints the landscape with that one suggestive line :

"How sweet the moonlight sleeps upon this bank."

Not a word about the trees or grasses or ponds or meadows ; not a word about the stillness of the night, the hushed winds, and the shining stars ; but do you not see them all ? Do they not rise up before your eyes as by magic ? Your realist would have put us

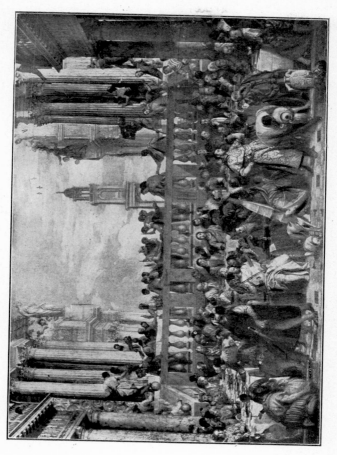

V.—PAOLO VERONESE, Marriage in Cana. Louvre, Paris.

to sleep with dreary descriptions of grass and groves and glittering dew-drops instead of the moonlight. And Shakespeare himself might have written a volume of description and still not roused us to his meaning so quickly as with that one suggestive line. The value of the sign in art, whether it be pictorial, sculptural, or literary, lies in its suggestive quality; and the "Sower" of Millet, the "Day" of Michael Angelo, and the moonlight of Shakespeare are merely so many suggestive signs.

Thus far our inquiry has extended no farther than the truth of nature—the truth of appearance as shown in realistic art. But there are other truths with which the picture has to do that perhaps call for a moment's consideration. The truth of history for which the public contends so valiantly need not detain us long. That Paolo Veronese and his contemporaries chose to garb the sacred characters of the "Marriage in Cana" (Plate 5) or "Moses saved from the Nile" (Plate 23), in Venetian costume, is matter of small importance. And it is of still less importance whether Christ and the Apostles show the Semitic cast of countenance or not. The intense reverence for local and ethnographical truth possessed by the Holman Hunts and Alma-Tademas of the art world would seem somewhat misplaced. No matter what care is bestowed upon the archæology, there is always something not quite true to the fact. And moreover, all art in all

times has pictured its own race, costume, and country.
It would not be worth much unless it did. The marble
gods of Greece are all Greek, the painted Madonnas of
Italy are all Italian. How otherwise would you have
it ? Marlowe's Mephistopheles talks English, and
Goethe's Mephistopheles talks German. What language should they talk ? When art deals with the past
it translates it into the present. It could not possibly
do otherwise. No Anglo-Saxon could feel, think, or
work like a Greek, simply because he is an Anglo-
Saxon.

There is another truth of far more consequence
than historical accuracy, and that is the truth of art.
This comes in here opportunely enough, for art-truth
is produced by the suggestive method of dealing with
facts which I have just been illustrating. The
method is absolutely essential to all strong work in
all departments. It is usually known in painting as
the " law of sacrifice " ; and you will find it in literature under the name of " dramatic force." We should
never have had such characters as Faust and Macbeth
had all the other characters in the plays been treated
with an importance equal to that of the heroes. Hamlet is an elevated Hamlet simply because the other
characters are subordinate characters, just as Corot's
light is light, because everything else in the picture
is sacrificed to it. There is no quarrel with truth to
nature in this truth to art. Great art seldom falsi-

fies, but it always selects, emphasizing some features and subordinating other features. It usually gives the large truths and merely implies the small ones. Millet in his "Sower" has no notion of telling you more than a few prominent facts about the man and his work. He shows a peasant, working under the shadow of a hill, working late in the evening, swinging and sowing with rhythmic motion of foot, hand, arm and body. It is matter of no importance whether he wears linen or woollen or cotton, whether his blouse has buttons upon it or not, whether his face is clean or not. The all-pervading truth of the picture lies in the swinging form of the sower, and to keep your attention upon that he omits everything else. The figure is but a suggestion, a something that stands as an equivalent for that man whom Millet thought should be recognized for his patience and fortitude of spirit, his nobility and dignity in the hard labor of life, his fine pictorial qualities as seen against the background of his native heath. That is the ulterior meaning which he would show us. The sign is true to the great truth of a sower, the meaning is true within the limits of pictorial creation, and finally the recording of it is true to the truth of art.

This method of procedure, wherein suggestion becomes such an important factor, implies two people in the work of art rather than one. The spectator must do his part as well as the artist. The latter suggests, the former takes up the suggestion and builds upon it. When Velasquez painted Christ on the cross, hanging there alone in the night, the head bowed forward on the breast, and the long dark hair falling over the face and half covering it, he did not think to obliterate the face—to take it out of the picture completely. He knew very well that the imagination of the spectator would go behind the veil and picture that face more vividly than he could paint it. What painter ever yet produced a wholly satisfactory face of Christ? Velasquez was wise in leaving it to the imagination of the spectator. How wise he was you can perhaps gather by contrasting his " Christ on the Cross " with the same subject by Léon Bonnat—one of the noblest of the latter-day realists. Bonnat simply took a dead body from the morgue and hung it upon a cross in the court-yard of the *École de Médecine*, and painted it exactly as he saw it. But it is not Christ; it is the dead body he took from the morgue. There is strain of arm and leg and torso, the anatomy is wrenched, the muscles are contorted, the veins are swollen. But there is no suggestion of anything that had been noble or exalted in the living. In fact there is not a suggestion of any kind. Everything is told and the spectator's imagination is not called upon. Realism has been pushed into the last ditch, and yet has produced only a sign standing for Christ on the cross, and not

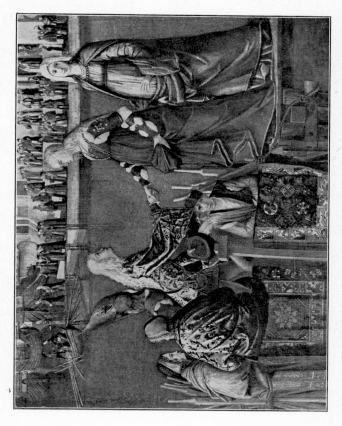

VI.—CARPACCIO, St. Ursula and Prince of England (detail). Academy, Venice.

the real thing—a sign which, in gaining an elaborate truth to fact, has lost its truth to art and its power of suggestion.

We may as well conclude then, without further illustration, that the exact portrayal of nature known as realism falls somewhat short of its mark. It may report and report, but it cannot realize. Light, air, hills, mountains, human beings and their habitations cannot be reproduced, but they may be translated through the medium of pigment and thus rendered intelligible to us. You may translate them "realistically" or you may translate them suggestively, but in either case it is the translation that you will have, and not the original. Each art—music, poetry, painting—has its peculiar method of translation, and we have called the result in each case a sign— a convention which we have agreed to recognize as meaning thus and so; but of course the signs in painting are not quite so arbitrary as in language or chemistry. The painting of a wave certainly looks more like a wave than the word "water," or the symbol H_2O. The sign has a certain resemblance to the original which gives a reason for the existence of realism and also adds to the confusion of those who would spin a theory of art; but the resemblance should not mislead us. The sign is still a sign, though in the one case it is representative and in the other case symbolic. Its meaning has not changed

in any way. The all-seeing eye of Osiris is not like
those speaking eyes in Van Dyck's portrait of " Cornelius Van der Geest" (Plate 3). One is more conventional than the other, but both are conventions.

It is not necessary that we should deny value to
this realistic art, even though we do not wholly accept it. The very endeavor to make the work faith-
ful to the original in every detail, though it may
hurt its deeper sentiment, cannot but result in good
workmanship ; and that in itself is always acceptable
and pleasurable. Indeed, bald realism, with nothing
else back of it, is seldom seen in art. The man, the
material, and the method are inextricably mixed together, so that the product always has more or less
individuality about it, or is decorative in form or
color, or expresses some thought or feeling of the
painter, or stands for something in subject. In any
event the well-made sign—even as a sign—is not to
be scorned. We shall see hereafter how it is distorted by the personal element, how it is twisted by
the imagination, how it is warped by the decorative
instinct ; but we are not to forget at any time that it
is but a symbol, merely a means of suggesting reality,
and not reality itself.

CHAPTER II

INDIVIDUALITY OR THE PERSONAL ELEMENT

THE fact that "the report about nature" which we have called "truth" varies with the reporter is of vital importance to us in comprehending the measure of exactness in the result. It is something that must be reckoned with in every thought, deed, and utterance, for its presence is potent in all human endeavor. Two astronomers, to use the accepted illustration, taking the time of the passage of a series of stars over the same meridian, will not precisely agree in their arithmetical results. However accurate, unbiassed, and mechanical in action they may seek to be, it happens that one takes the time earlier or later than the other. Consequently there is always a variation in the product, which has to be rectified by adding a constant. This is what is called the personal equation—a something we have heard about in literature and art as well as in science.

Perhaps you may remember that in the writing class of our youth when the motto, " Evil communications corrupt good manners," was given us as an example to copy, we all wrote the motto, and we all tried to follow the exact form of the copper-plate pattern before us; but somehow our performances differed one from another. In some the letters were large, in others they were small; the angle was flatter, the line was firmer, or the shading heavier. We used to think it merely a matter of practice, and fancied if we kept at it long enough we could ultimately write exactly like the copper-plate pattern. But I wonder if we thought quite correctly about that. Certainly there are thousands of people who have been writing all their lives and have had practice enough, but these are the ones that show the most marked variations from the model. Each one writes in a manner peculiarly his own. And these handwritings that vary so radically interest us very much. We see all sorts of striking peculiarities in them suggestive of their authors, and we even have so-called scientists who read character out of them, or into them, I will not say which. The cause of the variation is not far to seek. It is the personal element appearing in the work and influencing it. If we would get the same result in all handwritings we must eliminate the personal element or, if you please, reckon with the personal equation.

This quality which creates the variance in handwriting is met with even more positively in painting. For painting is, after all, only an elaborated picture-writing, more flexible, perhaps, than letter-writing, and, therefore, more easily bent by a personality; but in the main influenced by the same principles as regards the variation of the characters. We all write the letter " A " and they are all " A's," but each is different from the other, just as all landscape painters paint hills and trees and they are all hills and trees, yet each is different again. If three painters, say Turner, Rousseau, and Claude Monet, could be brought together and induced, each for himself, to paint a given tree, there can be no doubt that all three of the paintings would represent the tree and be true enough representations into the bargain; but they would not be at all like one another. The Turner would undoubtedly give the height, the branching outline, the grace and grandeur of the tree; but in flattened form, perhaps in silhouette against a yellow evening sky. In any event and under any circumstances we may be sure that it would be a Turnerian tree. And the Rousseau would be correspondingly true to Rousseau's peculiar point of view. It would probably have an emphasis of mass and volume; it would be as deep through as broad across, it would be firm in its rooting, massive in its trunk and branches, heavy in its foliage, rich in its coloring. But Claude Monet, painting the same tree, would not see the things that appealed to Turner and Rousseau, or if he did he would disregard them. He would overlook form and line and body, perhaps lose them entirely in studying the sunlight falling upon the foliage, in painting the colored reflections cast by sky and ground and water, in surrounding the tree with colored air and giving it a setting in an atmospheric envelope. Undoubtedly we should be able to recognize the original tree in any one of the three counterfeit presentments. Each would differ from the other and yet no one of them be false. There would be three different truths about the one tree—three different phases of the one fact. And undoubtedly we should be able to say just which painter painted each picture. How ? Because we should recognize in each the point of view peculiar to its maker—we should recognize the individuality of the painter.

If we consider this same tree as part of a landscape —consider it in connection with foreground, background, and sky—we shall see that the chance for the display of individuality is even greater. The choice of the painter as to how the tree shall be seen determines at the very start the character of the representation. If it is placed in the foreground and spreads in a pattern of branches and leaves high up against the sky, we have one phase of tree-truth, one kind of picture which may perhaps resemble, in a way, the work of Harpignies ; if it is placed in the middle distance, a shadowy form against a pale morning sky, with a feeling of heavy air and rising mists, we have another phase of truth, something which may represent Corot ; if it is seen in the far background against a yellow twilight sky, tall, dark, motionless, we have still another phase of truth which may stand for Daubigny. Any change in the position of the tree, any change in foreground or skyline, in light or reflection or atmosphere, would represent a new angle of vision and hence a new truth. And the preference of the painter for any particular phase of the manifestation, any particular truth, would exhibit what we have called his individuality.*

* This matter of personality and choice is well illustrated by Mr. La Farge in his "Considerations on Painting." He says (p. 71): "I remember myself, years ago, sketching with two well-known men, artists who were great friends, great cronies, asking each other all the time how to do this and how to do that! but absolutely different in the texture of their minds and in the result that they wished to obtain, so far as the pictures and drawings by which they were well known to the public are concerned.

"What we made, or rather, I should say, what we wished to note, was merely a memorandum of the passing effect upon the hills that lay before us. We had no idea of expressing ourselves or of studying in any way the subject for any future use. We merely had the intention to note this affair rapidly, and we had all used the same words to express to each other what we liked in it. There were big clouds rolling over hills, sky clearing above, dots of trees and water and meadow land below; and the ground fell away suddenly before us. Well, our three sketches were in the first place different in shape; either from

This preference for a peculiar point of view crops out very early in the painter's life. The students in an art class, drawing from the living model on the platform, and each one striving to follow that model literally, all show it. The sketches indicate by the placing of the figure upon the paper, the size of the figure, the height or depth of the shadows, the clearness or vagueness of the outline, that the personal element—individuality—is present, influencing and

our physical differences, or from a habit of drawing certain shapes of a picture, which itself usually indicates—as you know or ought to know—whether we are looking far or near. Two were oblong, but of different proportions; one was more nearly a square: the distance taken into the right and left was smaller in the *latter* case, and, on the contrary, the height up and down —that is to say, the portion of land beneath and the portion of sky above—was greater. In each picture the distance bore a different relation to the foreground. In each picture the clouds were treated with different precision and different attention. In one picture the open sky was the main intention of the picture. In two pictures the upper sky was of no consequence—it was the clouds and the mountains that were insisted upon. The drawing was the same—that is to say, the general make of things—but each man had involuntarily looked upon what was most interesting to him in the whole sight; and though the whole sight was what he meant to represent, he had unconsciously preferred a beauty or interest different from what his neighbors liked.

"The color of each painting was different—the vivacity of colors and tone, the distinctness of each part in relation to

VII.—BELLINI, Madonna and Saints. S. M. dei Frari, Venice.

practically dominating the work of everyone in the class-room. And this, too, in charcoal work, where the color problem is eliminated. Moreover, there are features of these charcoal sketches, aside from mere *technique*, that are equally interesting as indicative of the peculiar temperament behind the pencil. You cannot fail to be struck with the mood or spirit that creeps into each one of the drawings. On one paper the model looks pleasant, almost jovial, on another he will appear sad-faced or morose, on another, romantic as you might conceive a Wagner hero, or classic and insipid like a Canova marble, and on still another, gross, brutal, or perhaps fool-

the whole; and each picture would have been recognized any-where as a specimen of work by each one of us, characteristic of our names. And we spent on the whole affair perhaps twenty minutes. I wish you to understand again that we each thought and felt as though we had been photographing the matter before us. We had not the first desire of expressing *ourselves*, and I think would have been very much worried had we not felt that each one was true to nature. Of course there is no abso-lute nature, as with each slight shifting of the eye, involuntarily we focus more or less distinctly some part to the prejudice of others. And not only would this result have been the same if we had gone on painting, but had we made a drawing, had we made a careful representation or rapid note of what we saw by lines (that is to say, by an abstraction of the edges of the sur-faces that we saw), anyone could have told the names of the men who had done it."

ish-looking. It is not possible that the model could exhibit all these different moods. The variation is not in him. He presents the same stolid, tired front common to all models; the mood is added to him by the personality holding the charcoal.

We see the same variation among the works of older people—full-fledged artists, in the world of art. Nowhere is it more apparent than in the portrait, the one thing which might be thought to call for the elimination of the painter and a close fidelity to the facts of the original. But such is the power of preference that the painter almost invariably emphasizes certain features at the expense of others less interesting to him; or such is the warp of the vision that certain qualities appear abnormal, certain prominences appear unduly accentuated. There are portraits of the Duchess of Devonshire and of Mrs. Siddons (Plate 19) by both Reynolds and Gainsborough, but how very different they are! With Reynolds both of the characters are healthy, robust, good-natured, somewhat loud and stormy; with Gainsborough they are both delicate, subdued, refined, even melancholy. And think of the portraits in the Louvre of Francis I. by different hands, where only a slight thread of resemblance holds them together; or, better still, the portraits of Napoleon I., painted by the classic painters of his reign who believed in the utter effacement of the artist in favor of the facts before him. How very different in form, feature, mood, and character Napoleon appears in each picture. He is classic ; he is romantic ; he is thin, fat, amiable, moody, fiery, dreamy. David, Delaroche, Gros, no matter what their theories in art, could not keep themselves out of the representation. All that any one of them could do was to give his individual impression of the model before him. Necessarily each was tinctured by a predilection or a bias. It could not have been otherwise.

What is the cause of the variation in results to be seen in the portrait ? Why, for instance, do the photographs of Queen Victoria show substantially the same thing, while the portraits of her by paint- ers show different things ? Because the cameras are all made of practically the same material, have the same sensitiveness, and receive light in the same way; whereas men are not made of the same material, have not the same sensitiveness, and receive varying degrees of light according to their lucidity or ab- sorbent power, which is sometimes called genius. No two people are fashioned precisely after the same pattern. They vary in intellectual, emotional, and physical make-up. And let a painter strive as he may to record an exact fact before him, he cannot es- cape the action of his inherent faculties. These may be brighter, clearer, keener, than those of other painters, or they may be duller and feebler ; but at

least they are different, and he must use what nature
has given him. He was equipped originally to see
with his own eyes, think with his own brain, and
work with his own hands. Is it not very apparent
then that the eye may warp the vision and report
peculiarly to the brain, which in turn may tell the
hand to work thus and so ? And the result in art is
what ? Why, the individual view of one man ; or
nature passed through the alembic of that man's
personality.*

How shrewdly Coleridge discerned the truth in
that definition of art which I am so very fond of
quoting because of its exactness. He says that
painting is of "a middle quality between a thought
and a thing—the union of that which is nature with
that which is exclusively human." That is it, precisely. Art is an illusion of nature produced by a
personality. Human individuality must be in it because it cannot very well be kept out of it. What-

* "Our eyes, our ears, our sense of smell, of taste, differing
from one person to another, create as many truths as there are
men upon earth. And our minds, taking instructions from
these organs, so diversely impressed, understand, analyse, judge,
as if each of us belonged to a different race. Each one of us,
therefore, forms for himself an illusion of the world ; and the
writer (the painter, too) has no other mission than to reproduce
faithfully this illusion, with all the contrivances of art that he
has learned and has at his command."—GUY DE MAUPASSANT,
Fortnightly Review, March, 1888, p. 366.

VIII —CORREGGIO, Mystic Marriage of St. Catherine. Louvre, Paris.

ever we do, we speak ourselves. For a time we may act a part—copy someone else—but sooner or later the mask falls and we stand revealed in the form and manner nature designed for us. We are all peculiar in our make-up physically, mentally, and æsthetically. To the European all Chinamen look alike, and possibly to Chinamen all Americans look alike ; but we know there is a variation. We may seem as like as peas in a peck measure, but we differ in the conformation of a wrinkle. Out of a hundred acquaintances on the street how easy it is to recognize each one apart from his fellows. There is a peculiarity in look or walk or bearing that betrays the man. And of those hundred acquaintances each one, as we have already noted, writes in an individual way and you are able to distinguish the handwritings by the variations in the muscular action of the hands. Suppose you should have read to you extracts from a hundred famous authors, do you think you would have much difficulty in recognizing Shakespeare from Victor Hugo, Carlyle from Cardinal Newman, or Walter Scott from Swinburne ? Could you possibly mistake an essay by Bacon for an essay by Macaulay, or could you by any chance confuse a sermon by Canon Liddon with a sermon by Spurgeon ? I think not, for the individuality of mind and thought is even more positive and assertive than the individuality of the physical presence.

If you are acquainted with pictures you can enter a gallery in which you have never been before, and standing in the middle of the room you can pick out at a distance the Corots, the Diazes, the Monets, the Millets, the Delacroixs—yes, the Rubenses, the Van Dycks, the Holbeins, and the Titians. And this, too, with a large degree of accuracy. You are very likely to be right in your ascriptions. Why? Because you know the artistic individualities of each one of those painters—know just how they see, think, feel, and paint—as you know the personal appearance of an acquaintance upon the street, or recognize his handwriting upon the face of an envelope. When the question of a picture's attribution comes up, when it is of moment whether a work is by a Raphael or a Perino del Vaga, by a Velasquez or a Mazo, there is an unconscious appeal made to the spirit of the picture. And this quite aside from a question of *technique,* aside from any Morellian theory of tools or methods or models. Does the work reflect the spirit of Raphael? Is the impress of his individuality to be felt in the canvas? If it is genuine, yes; if by a follower, no. The sugary little "Reading Magdalene" in the Dresden Gallery, so long attributed to Correggio, gives not the slightest hint of that great painter's individuality; the alleged portrait of Raphael by himself in the Louvre shows all the blundering stupidity of Bacchiacca.

Whether master or follower, the painter cannot disguise himself effectively. Back of the work we feel the presence of the worker. The great artists fashion their art after their own thoughts, and that which they love the best or feel the deepest speaks out from the canvas until at last we recognize the poet in his poem, the sculptor in his marble, the painter in his picture.

These qualities of individuality in art are much like the same qualities in real life, and we may perhaps fancy in the picture that which we find admirable in the personal acquaintance. For instance, the traits of frankness and straightforwardness which we all love in a friend, are they not just as apparent in Carpaccio the painter ? And just as lovable ? The way in which Carpaccio tells the history of St. Ursula or St. George—so frank in spirit and yet so cunning of hand—reminds one somehow of a chapter from Sir John Maundevile or Roger of Wendover. How *naif* he is with his gorgeously robed Venetians (Plate 6) ! How earnest he is about the dignity of the types, the nobility of the faces, the sobriety of the action ! His sincerity is as great as that of Giotto, and his absolute unconsciousness—his lack of egotism— as apparent as that of Fra Angelico. At the foot of the " Presentation " in the Venetian Academy is that little angel playing upon a lute which you have all seen in reproductions so many times. You must

have noticed that the angel was not playing for public applause, but for the glory of the Madonna standing above. There is no thought of you or of me, or
anyone outside of the Madonna and the group of
saints. That quality of unconsciousness we need
not attribute to angels. It is no characteristic of
theirs so far as we know; but it was a quality of
Victor Carpaccio, the Venetian painter.

Think for a moment of the "Madonna and
Saints" in the sacristy of the Frari by Giovanni
Bellini (Plate 7). How absolutely honest and un-
abashed she looks! This is not the Madonna of
Sorrows, not the pathetic Madonna of Botticelli;
but a purely human mother, proud of her boy—a
mother and not ashamed. And the little cherubs
playing on musical instruments at the foot of the
throne, how child-like they are with their serious
faces, their little fat cheeks and round childish
legs! Everything in and about the picture tells
you of the sane, healthy mind and art of Giovanni
Bellini. The Madonna's honesty is Bellini's honesty; the view of the cherubs as merely beautiful
and graceful children of this earth is Bellini's view;
yes, the gorgeous coloring of the patterned background, the superb architecture, even the rich orna-
mentation of the framing are Bellini's taste. We
cannot, if we would, escape the man. He is omni-
present in his work. Why should he not be? The

story in literature becomes fascinating through the personality and skill of the story-teller; why should not the theme in art be beautiful through the individuality and skill of the painter?

Those of you who have been in Rome and have studied in the Sistine Chapel know with what a feeling of awe the great figures on the ceiling inspire one. You feel the presence of a mighty spirit within the walls, hovering about the vaulted space, in the very air of the chapel itself. What is it? Surely, nothing in the architecture or the lighting of the chapel; nothing in the subjects of the frescoes, for they are familiar subjects in art. It is the impress of a commanding individuality that you feel. Michael Angelo lives here in his pictures. Those great forms of the Prophets and Sibyls lost in thought, brooding over the evil of their days, isolated in their grandeur, living on in gloomy solitude, how very like they are to what we know of Michael Angelo himself! Notice the fore-shortened hand and arm of the "Delphic Sibyl" (Plate 21) and how symbolic of strength it is, how like to the power that lay in the arm, hand, and mind of the master himself! Follow the outline of the figure of the newly created Adam —perhaps the grandest piece of drawing in all pictorial art—and how that summarized, synthetized line speaks the comprehensive grasp, scope, knowledge, and plastic feeling of the great draughtsman.

So it is that individuality creeps into the work of art and tinges the whole character of it. Of the thousands of pictures we pass before in public galleries the great majority of them are merely records of individual tastes, beliefs, aspirations, emotions. In other words they are partial autobiographies of the painters, showing countless moods of human nature. Some of them are grave, some gay, some refined, some fierce, some grandiloquent, some resplendent. Almost every shade of sentiment and feeling, almost every quality personal to the man, can be recorded in art. And this, without premeditated thought, without extravagant effort, without conscious action. The note of a bird discloses its kind not more unconsciously than the hand of the artist tells the quality of the man.

If all the lives of Rembrandt were swept out of existence we should still be able to reconstruct his individuality from his pictures. His must have been an intensely emotional nature. For not in the "Supper at Emmaus" alone do we find the sorrow-stained face. The portraits of himself are only too often sad-eyed and passion-wrung; and there is in the National Gallery, London, one of his portraits of an old woman with a lace cap and a white ruff (No. 775 of the Catalogue) that shows a mouth and chin quivering with emotion, and eyes that seem red with weeping. The man was tragic in his passionate power. He could not suppress it. Even when he laughs you feel that he is doing so to avoid a moan. We have little record of the life of Giorgione, but from two or three of his pictures we know he must have been quite the reverse of Rembrandt. His " Madonna," at Castelfranco (Plate 24) and his " Concert," in the Louvre (in Giorgione's style if not by his hand), tell us his Theocritean nature— loving life for its pastoral beauty, revelling in sunshine, shadow and color, careless of everything but the pure joy of living. We know still less about Correggio, but his pictures (Plate 8) say to us that he was of a similar faun-like nature—a man who grew eloquent over the grace and charm of women and children, and cared little or nothing for the religious themes of his time.

And so we might go on down the long line of paintings, recognizing in each picture the note that harmonized with the painter's individuality. What, for instance, is more apparent than the charm of Corot as seen in his landscapes (Plate 9) ? His pictures delight us by their alluring qualities of calmness, radiance, unity. They are fair dreams of splendor in which dawn and twilight glow through a silver veil of atmosphere, in which the winds are hushed and the waters are stilled and that peace that passeth understanding, that joy which is beyond price, have fallen upon the dwellers in Arcadia.

Charm in its various manifestations has been the possession of not a few painters. Many of the Italians—Leonardo, Filippino, Lorenzo Costa, Sodoma—possessed it; the eighteenth century Englishmen—Wilson, Gainsborough, Romney—were not without it; and the modern landscape painters—Daubigny (Plate 16), Cazin, Homer Martin, Tryon—have shown it in almost all their work. Serenity is a quality allied to charm in that it is restful and hence an attractive feature. All the great men possessed it. Raphael was primarily its exponent in Rome as Giorgione in Venice. The superb repose of Titian and Velasquez is akin to it; and the calm of the Parthenon marbles is part of the same spirit. Refinement is another characteristic that may be shown in painting as readily as in print. It has nothing to do with fine furniture, fine clothes, and a pretty face. A picture may possess all the elegance of the latest fashion and still be the epitome of vulgarity. Refinement in art means the delicacy, the distinction of feeling that a painter may possess and show in his work. Terburg made it apparent in so simple a thing as the drawing of a chair leg or a table-cloth, Chardin showed it in his pots, pans and dishes, and it is obvious to the most obtuse in Van Dyck's portraits of men, women and children. (Plate 18.) A tenderness of feeling as well as of touch has been exhibited many times in painting. Dürer shows

IX.—COROT, Landscape. Louvre, Paris.

it in his "Christ on the Cross" (Plate 10), and Botticelli suggests it in almost every picture he ever painted, whether sacred or profane (Plate 29). Just so with sensitiveness, which we see so beautifully shown in the portraits by Lorenzo Lotto, or impetuosity as revealed in the great dramatic canvases by Tintoretto, or liveliness as seen in the garden scenes of Pater or the soubrette figures of Fragonard. The words describe the spirit of the pictures and they also suggest the nature of the painter.

And note too, if you please, that the disagreeable and unpleasant qualities of the individual crop out in painting as in social life. How many modern painters do we know whose works exhale the atmosphere of the Folies-Bergères and the Bal Bullier. Their subjects may be pure enough or refined enough ; they may picture decent people, high life, and fashionable surroundings, and yet do it with an unwholesome mind and a tell-tale brush. There are painters (their names need not be mentioned) who cannot paint a lady without showing the *cocotte*, nor a gentleman without showing the blackguard, nor a child without showing a certain sophistication—a precocious knowledge of evil—altogether unhappy. The coarseness of Jan Steen or Brouwer may be passed over as incidental to his time. It is coarse, but neither vulgar nor immoral. But not so the brutality of the modern cosmopolite who boasts so openly in his pictures that he has no faith in the virtue of women nor the respectability of men.

And what vulgarity we see in every modern exhibition, whether held in Chicago, London, or Paris! Painters there are, born and bred no one knows where or how, who depict Oxford professors or statesmen with the air and attitude of flunkies, or duchesses with the smirk of shop-girls. And painters there are, too, who, assuming for their characters the elegance of luxury, paint pictures that seem to reek of perfumes, scented soaps, and manicured finger-nails. Such men seem to leave an unhappy impress upon the trees and mountains, and their point of view vulgarizes the blue sky. They may be very brilliant handlers of the brush—indeed they are often excellent craftsmen—but their vision is sadly warped and their minds are tainted. There are, for instance, few workmen more fascinating in craftsmanship than Goya. He could paint beautifully and convincingly, but when you go to Spain and see the mass of his painting you will be surprised at the blood and flame and brutality of it. The man's mind, at times, was hideous, unearthly, poisoned with bitterness. On the contrary take the work of Carlo Dolci or Sassoferrato and you meet with supersaturated sentimentality and mawkishness. Neither was a bad painter for his age and people, but his mental attitude was lacking in force—perhaps had not enough brutality about it.

And human conceit exudes as readily from the painter's brush as from the writer's pen. You have no trouble in recognizing conceit in a book. It is only too apparent. And yet all that clever painting, that *bravura* of the brush, that elaborate flourish of the little men who try to make a great noise and attract attention to themselves, is mere pictorial conceit. And there is so much of it in modern painting. It seems sometimes as though the exhibitions were more than half made up of flippant displays of dexterity, which have no other aim than to show how very clever the painter can be and still avoid seriousness.

But I need not stop longer to discuss disagreeable characteristics in art. They are not our quest in any sense and they are referred to here merely to suggest anew that the man—be he weak or strong, good or bad, noble or ignoble, serious or flippant— eventually appears in his work. Individuality will speak out though the individual may not be aware of it.

And this is as it should be. The disagreeable personality misleads for only a short time. Eventually it is ignored in art as in social life. And that which is really good in painting is the better for the strong individuality behind it. The frank statement of personal feeling or faith, the candid autobiography, has added more to the real knowledge of life, and has done more to show people how to live, than all the long volumes of scientific history, of which we have enough and to spare in every library. When a person speaks of himself he knows his subject at least, and can speak of it truly ; but when he speaks of dead-and-gone Alexanders and Cæsars, he is speculating in "perhapses" and "possiblys." And so in painting, when a person paints what he individually sees and is impressed by, he is likely to produce something worthy of attention ; but when he takes up some formula of truth laid down by a school or a camera he is merely repeating a something he has not seen, and simulating a feeling he has not known.

Even the positive assertion—the insistent assertion—of one's own view is often welcome in art. I think we all like the self-reliance, the steadfastness of belief of the individual—assuming, of course, that he is right and not therefore merely obstinate. When Delacroix was opposed by the classic painters of his day because he saw nature in patches of color and light, instead of in outlines and linear extensions, he declared defiantly : "The whole world cannot prevent me from seeing things in my own way." He insisted upon it that his "way" was a right way, even if different from that of Ingres. He was seeking to picture something peculiar to himself, in a manner entirely his own. Listen to him again: "I am at my window and I see the most beautiful landscape; the idea of a line never comes into my head. The lark sings, the river glitters, the foliage murmurs; but where are the lines that produce these charming sensations?" There you have the individual point of view, and in the 1840's it was a very unusual view. It was the self-reliant quality of the man, which enabled him to discard the outworn conception of his contemporaries and create a something new; and it is largely by the creative faculty arising from the desire to say something new, that we distinguish genius from mediocrity or eccentricity.

For you know that people whom we call "queer" can be just as individual as others, and yet not accomplish anything of importance. There is an individuality of genius which consists in original impression and statement; and there is an eccentricity of foolishness which produces only the bizarre. It is not difficult, however, to distinguish between them. For, as we have already noted, true individuality is always creative. It builds up, has a definite aim, proceeds to a definite goal; whereas, eccentricity is disordered, disposed to be meaningless, inclined to produce brilliant fragments that have no connection with each other. We see the same qualities exhibited in the social characters of real

life, and gossip says that such a man is a " genius "
or that another is " eccentric." It is by some outward manifestation or action, akin to expression in
painting, that gossip arrives at its conclusion ; and
it is usually a correct conclusion.

Then, too, there are painters who lose their individuality—throw it aside to take up with the view of
some other person who seems to have achieved more
popularity. The majority of men break down in
their ideals long before they are old. They may
have possessed talent, and given voice to it in early
years ; but it has been unnoticed, perhaps unheard.
They may have had impressions of their own ; but
perhaps they have not proved attractive to the
masses, or have not received the immediate recognition to which their producers perhaps thought them
entitled. Then they make the irretrievable mistake
of trying to follow someone whose impressions seem
to be in public demand. It may be that they follow
Raphael or Titian or Velasquez ; but no matter how
good a painter they may choose for a model, they
have already committed artistic suicide. No one in
this world of ours ever became great by echoing the
voice of another, repeating what that other has said.
Are there not countless illustrations of this—illustrations by whole schools of painters and sculptors in
the history of art ? What was the art of Rome, following as it did the art of Greece ? What was the

art of those who followed Michael Angelo, Raphael, and Correggio? What was the seventeenth-century art of France, following that of Italy? What was David and classicism, following ancient Rome? What is to-day the value of all these French peasants and Seine landscapes for which Millet and Corot set the patterns, and in the imitation of which America has contributed her modicum of strength? It is all a vapid and somewhat meaningless copying that may furnish canvases to hide a break in the wall-paper of a drawing-room, but as original art counting for naught. And why? Simply because it lacks in individuality—lacks in originality of aim and statement.

That last statement may be almost as fittingly applied to those who literally imitate nature as to those who imitate some other painter. It adds nothing to our store of knowledge, nothing to our appreciation of beauty, to have the painter reproducing line upon line and shade upon shade and color upon color the exact scene from nature. "A mere copier of nature," says Sir Joshua, "can never produce anything great; can never raise and enlarge the conceptions or warm the heart of the spectator." The insistence upon fact crowds the man out of the picture. Individuality does not appear, except perhaps in a manner of handling which shows the artisan rather than the artist. The Denners and Meissoniers and Gerard Dous have no individualities that you can

trace in their pictures. You know they were workmen and that is about all. Realism with them, as
with all devoted followers of the "truth to nature"
theory, is an attempt at eliminating the personal
element, an attempt at approximating the working
of a machine. Of course the attempt is never fully
realized, but it may be carried far enough to destroy
whatever might have been stimulating or exalted in
the picture.

And just so with those painters who produce academic art or, as it has been known for many years,
classic art. It is based upon an abstraction, an ideal
taken from memories or remains of Greek art; and it
is produced, in a scholastic way, according to an un-
written canon of academic proportions. Bouguereau
and Lefebvre are the last notable exponents of it in
France, and excellent craftsmen they are, too; but
somehow their pictures always remind one of the
book-keeper's handwriting. They are very good as
official handicraft—excellent drawings after a model
—but they seem to lack character. They have no
more force than the pretty girl on the outside of the
handkerchief box, for whose existence, indeed, they
are largely responsible. The want of stamina and
vitality in their pictures may be accounted for readily
enough, because again the man is absent. The work
is mapped out by rule and done by academic precept.
As for the feeling and the enthusiasm of the painter

X.—DÜRER, Christ on the Cross. Dresden Gallery.

they are not apparent, and the product is accordingly colorless, mechanical, somewhat insipid.

This academic art is just as impersonal as the so-called realistic art, but, of course, neither of them is impersonal through the ignorance of their producers. It is a part of their creed that the painter should be absolutely " wiped out of the canvas," and that the picture is complete only when the means of its production (including the painter) are no longer apparent in the work. The realist believes that nature is above all, the most beautiful of all beauties, and that the best the painter can do is to copy her in all humility of spirit. The academician believes that the academic rule—the consensus of tradition as to what constitutes beauty in art—is better than any one painter's eyes and hand, and that the best the moderns can do is to follow the greatest of the ancients, namely, the Greeks. But we have seen the impossibility of absolute realism in art and we can imagine the futility of copying an art of the past to be applied to a people of the present. In practice neither kind of art has proved satisfying. The insistence upon academic and realistic formulas has always led to denials and revolts. The bitterest quarrels in art have hinged upon whether painting should be personal or impersonal, whether a man should follow a model, a rule, an inexorable law, or whether he should create and be a law unto himself. We have been told many times that the struggles and neglect of the Delacroixs, the Corots, and the Millets were due to the stupid public that refused to recognize them ; but on the contrary, it was the stupid academicians of the *École des Beaux Arts* who would not understand them and denounced them. The protestants did not conform to the academic standard—they did not recite by rote.

Great art never has admitted a law ; it will not be bound down to a model or a formula ; it will not tolerate a rule if it can gain by breaking it. It is primarily the expression of man's delight in what he sees or feels, and every man must express himself in his own way and in his own language. Indeed, the longer we ponder over the subject the surer we are to agree in substance with Véron that " of every work of art we may truly say that its chief value consists in the personal character of its author."

These different kinds of art—realism, classicism, individualism—we frequently hear spoken of in metaphysical terms, which one hesitates to use for fear of producing confusion. When a person begins talking about " the real " and " the ideal," " the objective " and " the subjective," we are at once all at sea ; because those words seem to have been used to define everything in the art world, and no two definitions mean quite the same thing. But as we may consider impersonal art hereafter, perhaps it is as well to say that it is often referred to as objective art. That is to say, it is as much as possible a realization of the object or thing painted. It is the outer view, seeing things beautiful in external nature. Personal art, on the contrary, is usually referred to as subjective art. It is the inner view, seeing things beautiful in the mind's impression or the heart's emotion. The interest in the one case centres in the representation of the model; in the other case it emanates from the expression of the painter himself.

Of course, the work of art does not necessarily hinge upon this question of personality or impersonality in the picture. There is the decorative quality that counts for much; there is something in subject that may be of importance; and there is, too, the style of the work, which may be strong enough to overcome other and perhaps detracting features. We have not yet finished with our consideration of the picture, and are not yet ready to draw a conclusion. It may be that conclusions in art are the better for not being "drawn" too rigidly. The arts which depend so largely upon varying personalities and temperaments cannot be summed up and proved with the exactness of a mathematical problem. Sometimes from a mass of illustrations one may extract a few general principles, and if we succeed in doing that we shall be taking at least one step forward in the appreciation of art.

CHAPTER III

IMAGINATION OF THE ARTIST

IN our consideration of the varying points of view held by painters we have been placing the responsibility for the variations upon the human eye. The argument has been that people see differently one from another; and from that you have perhaps inferred that there is a difference in the construction of eyes. It is true that there may be a physical difference through imperfections of sight, as when one is near-sighted or has some astigmatism or is color-blind. But defective vision does not account for the individual view and is not a factor in the present consideration. The physical make-up of the eye may be assumed as practically the same with all men. The retina is merely a mirror which receives an impression of a scene or object. But the reception of the impression is not the beginning and the end of seeing. The complete act requires a mental recognition of what is seen—requires perception. The word "seeing" then should be understood as meaning not only the mirror-work of the retina, but the perception of that work by the mind.

In the matter of perception there may be differences among men and still be no great display of what we have called individuality. Some people perceive much while others seem almost blind. You know that the eyes of an unconscious person may be wide open, with the retinas mirroring everything, and yet the mind perceiving nothing. And so people who are quite conscious may look at things and not see them. The blue shadows cast upon the snow were, no doubt, seen centuries ago, but not perceived until the very recent time of the impressionists ; and the Hebrews must have seen the difference between the blue sky and white light as the Greeks the difference between the hues of yellow and orange without being aware of what they saw.*

The eyes of the workmen who select the skeins of colors for the Gobelin tapestries are physically not different from other eyes, but they recognize scores of tints and shades that your perception and mine cannot grasp at all. This is usually assumed to be the result of the training of the eye ; but the eye cannot be trained like the hand. It is passive and receptive ; not active. The training is that of the mind to note the sensations of the eye. So far as keenness and clearness of vision are concerned, I

* A most interesting discussion of what the ancient peoples knew of lights and colors is to be found in Franz Delitzsch, *Iris, Studies in Color*, etc., Edinb., 1899.

know of no people more remarkable than the Papago and Yuma Indians, and yet in the Colorado Desert I have frequently called their attention to the lilac shadows upon sand-banks, to the pink and yellow hazes of sunset, to the blue-steel glow of mountain walls at noonday, without ever finding one of them to nod an affirmative. They know form, outline, movement, and crude color in large masses, but the refinements of hue, the subtleties produced by light-and-shade, though doubtless seen by the eye, are not recognized by the mind.

Much of the fumbling with the paint brush found in present-day pictures is no doubt due to an inadequate perception of the model. In the studios you will often hear painters declaring that they can see things clearly enough, but their " technique bothers them ; " they cannot get their fingers or canvases or colors or brushes to work properly. But the trouble is really more fundamental. It is their lack of perception that bothers them. Whenever a person in art or in literature knows his subject thoroughly there is no difficulty about words or lines or colors to express it. Men like Leibl and Meissonier, who see acutely every feature before them, are not worried by a want of technical expression. That their work, with all its cleverness of hand and keenness of vision, is somewhat mechanical—lacking in inspiration —may suggest that clearness of view is not the only requisite of art. It is, no doubt, a valuable accomplishment with any painter, and yet if the picture tells only a tale of facts it has fallen short of the highest aim. Keen eyes and a clever hand will not take the place of that vital quality of all great art— the imagination of the artist. For the imagination is, perhaps, the very essence of artistic seeing.

In the ordinary acceptation of the word the imagination is little more than the image-making power —the ability to see a thing in the mind's eye. We all of us have the power in some degree and can summon up scenes out of the past at will, travelling fair lands that we have not known for years, and seeing faces that have long been shut away in the grave. In boyhood, when the imagination is active and disposed to build air-castles, you doubtless saw yourself many times as the hero of imaginary deeds of daring, carrying off the beautiful princess from the enchanted castle, just as older people like Dumas saw the adventurous D'Artagnan, and painters like Rossetti saw the Blessed Damosel leaning from the gold bar of Heaven with eyes far

" Deeper than the depth
Of waters stilled at even ;
She had three lilies in her hand,
And the stars in her hair were seven."

Such flights of the imagination as these, you will understand, are connected and associated with "memories," of which we shall have something to say further on ; but they are not the less connected with the image-making power.

When the object or the cause is present before us instead of far back in the past, the process of image-making is not radically different. We see and comprehend by an image in the mind. A portrait painter, to take an example at once from pictures, does not exercise his imagination upon a sitter by conceiving him as a great lawyer, a great poet, or a great general. He does not think of him in connection with what he has done or has been. Nor does he eliminate the Mr. Hyde from his appearance, and give only the good Dr. Jekyll part of him. That would not be pictorial imagination so much as pictorial falsehood, the popular belief to the contrary notwithstanding. What he really does is to look over his sitter with an eye to his exterior appearance ; then he imagines him as he would look upon canvas, and finally he takes up a brush and tries to paint the image he sees in his mind. That image in his mind is his conception, his idea—yes, his ideal, if you choose to use that badly misused word. His imagination has rounded and shaped the appearance, and just as is the weakness or the strength of his image-making power so will be the weakness or

XI.—TURNER, The Fighting Téméraire. National Gallery, London.

strength of his portrait, the execution, for the present, being disregarded.

But now observe, if you please, that the painter, in looking over his sitter, does not necessarily see him as the lens of a camera might see him. The imagination may insist upon his seeing less accurately and more positively—perhaps abnormally. The man before him may have a peculiar breadth of forehead, an unusual width between the eyes, a hollowness in the cheek, a pinched look in the nose and mouth ; or it may be he has a foxy eye, a puffed cheek, a flabby, vicious-looking lip, and a sensual-looking hand. These may be the very features that the imagination seizes upon and emphasizes. Then when the painter takes up his brush he paints these features strongly because they appeal to him strongly. And what is the result ? The look—perhaps in the one case scholarly and thoughtful, like Van Dyck's "Cornelius Van der Geest" (Plate 3), or in the other case crafty-looking like Velasquez's "Innocent X" (Plate 13)—the look that betrays the character of the sitter appears in the picture, appears more strongly emphasized than in the original ; and all through the proper exercise of the imagination.

The pictorial imagination almost always lays emphasis upon prominent features, and may at times distort them without falsifying them as art. The very first act, the seeing of things pictorially—that is, as they would appear in a picture rather than as they appear in real life—is necessarily a translation if not a free rendering. Everyone knows that George Morland, who saw English tavern-life cut up into beautiful pictures and hanging upon the walls, did not see accurately or scientifically ; but he certainly saw pictorially and imaginatively. The actual would have left us cold, where the imaginative excites admiration.

We can see something akin to this even in the work of the camera. The ordinary photograph of a flock of sheep is prosaic enough, but we have all seen photographs of sheep taken when the camera was a little "off-focus," when some of the sheep at the side did not get into the line of light and were somewhat distorted and magnified in bulk. In this " off-focus " view the sheep immediately become pictorial in appearance, and we notice how much like Millet's sheep they look. Of course the unusual appearance is caused by a perversion of light in the camera, but I do not know that Millet's sheep are not caused by a perversion of sight in the man. Genius is supposed to be closely allied to insanity ; and imagination may be allied to distortion.

Certainly there is in the pictorial view something of the distorted view. A modern athlete in the gymnasium is a very different athlete from those that writhe upon the ceiling of the Sistine Chapel. Did

not Michael Angelo's imagination see the model abnormally, and thus persuade his hand to emphasize
all the powerful attributes ? A running horse as
seen by the instantaneous camera is no doubt accurate enough in all respects, save the sense of motion.
He does not run. The camera arrests his flight,
holds him poised in air momentarily. But Fromentin's imagination, as shown in his pictures, saw the
horse running, saw him distorted, drawn out in body
from head to tail. You know from the report of the
camera, again, how human beings fall through the
air in jumping, diving, plunging ; but what a different report you get from Tintoretto's fall of the
damned in his "Last Judgment." There is a tre-
mendous rain of elongated bodies falling from
heaven to hell. The exaggeration of the imagination is here most apparent, but the result is won-
derfully effective. We are made to feel that the
bodies are really falling.

The reason for the pictorial distortion in the instances cited must be obvious enough. There is no
great attempt to present things precisely as they are
in nature. We have already arrived at the conclusion that this would be impossible. The object pre-
sented to the imagination is sought to be *re-presented*
by the sign or symbol, and it requires the radical
translation, possibly the distortion of the sign or
symbol to show the imaginative conception. **What**

was the actual bulk of the battle-ship Téméraire I do not know, but I feel quite sure that Turner in painting that vessel (Plate 11) saw it in exaggerated proportions, saw it lifted high out of the water, its height additionally emphasized by the smallness of the towing tug. In the same way Claude and Poussin saw trees and groves of phenomenal height and thickness (Plate 26), as Courbet saw sea waves of astounding bulk, and Claude Monet saw exaggerated lights and colors upon the towers of Rouen Cathedral. The exaggeration is quite within the province of the imagination—quite necessary to all imaginative art. It is more apparent in some painters than in others, and yet is not the less existent in almost all pictorial expression. From the caricature of the child to the conception of the skilled artist there is apparently only a step. The boy in school who draws the face of a companion on the fly-leaf of his book, giving it perverted features and a wide smile of countenance, is distorting the sign to convey a certain ludicrous impression ; but the Egyptian sculptor who carved the mysterious smile upon the face of the Sphinx—that face which under burning suns and midnight stars has looked out across the silence for so many centuries—was using the distorted sign, too, using it imaginatively to tell people his idea of the majesty and serenity of the sun-god Harmachis.

But however the imagination may distort, it cannot originate anything entirely new nor create anything outside of human experience. We are sometimes led to think, by the common use of the word "imagination," that it can

"Body forth the forms of things unknown,"

as Shakespeare has put it; but it must be apparent that "out of nothing, nothing comes," and that it is impossible to make a body from things unknown. All the originality of all the great originals in the world's history goes no further than the dividing up or the adding to of things already known. You may make a novel landscape perhaps by shutting out the sky with a high sky-line, or you may make an angel by adding bird wings to a human form ; but you cannot make an absolutely new form or create one thing that has not some basis in human life or experience. To be sure, you may bring to mind the image of a character in fiction or poetry— Sir Galahad or Roland of Brittany or Amadis de Gaul, for instance—but after all your image is based upon some previous memories of knights in armor. Just so with the likeness of Christ. There is no authentic record of how he looked, either in picture or worded description, and the type of Christ which we accept to-day has been derived from Italian art, which in turn received and blended together two

types—one from the Eastern Church at Constantinople and one from the Western Church at Rome.
As for the abnormal creations that seem at times
quite original—the witches of " Macbeth," the fair-
ies of " Midsummer Night's Dream," the water ba-
bies of Kingsley, the elves and gnomes and dwarfs of
Grimm—they are all founded upon the distortion of
the human figure. The wonders of the " Thousand
and One Nights," the City of Brass, the diamond
windows, the hanging gardens, the genii of the
clouds, are not different as regards the manner of
their construction. Animal life too, is made monstrous by the quips of the fancy, but again the dragons are all snake-formed and the goblins all bat-
winged ; the centaur is a combination of man and
horse, and Ariosto's hippogriff is the familiar winged
Pegasus of Greece translated into Italian.

In the first exercise of the imagination (that is, by
division) we shall find that the mind conceives a part
of an object, for instance, as of sufficient value to
stand by itself. This is separated from the whole,
magnified by emphasis, and finally handed forth as
an entity—a new creation, if you please. We can see
this well exemplified in poetry, where Keats, for instance, not wishing to describe the entire winter
landscape on the Eve of St. Agnes, isolates a few
features of the scene and makes them do service
for all.

XII.— ANTONELLO DA MESSINA, Portrait of a Man.   Louvre, Paris.

" Ah, bitter chill it was—
The owl for all his feathers was a-cold,
The hare limped trembling through the frozen grass,
And silent was the flock in woolly fold.''

Here we have an owl, a hare, and a flock of sheep
magnified out of all proportion as regards their importance in the landscape, and standing by themselves as symbols of a cold winter night. But the
suggestiveness of these features is very effective,
very complete—much more so than if an elaborate
description had been given of snow and icicle, moonlight and sleigh-bells. Claude Monet, when he
wishes to show a winter morning on the Seine, does
it with very few objects. There are silent ranks of
trees, a foggy air congealed to hoar-frost, the swollen
river with floating ice crunching and jostling its way ;
and that is all. But again what an effective winter
morning ! The heat of summer he describes just as
summarily by cutting off a square of vivid sunshine
falling on a wheatstack, exaggerating it in brilliancy
of color and light, and allowing it to stand in lieu of
a whole landscape. Corot is not different in thought
and method. He throws all his strength upon light
along the hills of morning or evening, and every detail of grass and tree and human being is sacrificed
to it (Plate 9).

There are many ways in which the dividing imagination deals with the figure in painting. The model may be treated as part of a group, as an object in landscape, as a whole-length portrait in a room, as a knee-piece, as a half-length, as a bust, or as a head alone. Nothing could be further removed from the actual than a man's head shown in profile on a coin, but what imaginative art the Greeks made of their coinage ! And what superb heads—superb in their character—the Pisani put upon their medals ! How well each head suggested the whole man ! And was there ever a more virile, living personality, ever a man with a more lion-hearted look, than Antonello da Messina pictured in the head and shoulders of that unknown Italian in the Louvre (Plate 12) ? Byron's ghost portrait of Nimroud as he appears to Sardanapalus in a dream is more colossal, but it is not more intense or forceful than Antonello's, save as language is always more definite than pigment. Here it is :

> " The features were a giant's and the eye
> Was still yet lighted ; his long locks curled down
> On his vast bust whence a huge quiver rose
> With shaft-heads feathered from the eagle's wing
> That peeped up bristling through his serpent hair."

To match in bulk such an imaginative picture, we should have to go back to the great king-headed bulls that flank the portals of the Assyrian palaces, or the colossal pharaonic figures in granite that symbolize the Egyptian kings.

Sculpture affords many good illustrations of parts detached from the whole and magnified by the imagination into separate creations. The Colleoni statue at Venice comes to mind instantly. The great commander and his horse have been taken out of battle and placed upon a pedestal, yet, isolated as it is, how the statue tells the irresistible strength, the pushing power of both man and horse ! The " Water Nymphs " of Jean Goujon are separated again in panels, they tell no connected story ; but the serpentine grace of the figures, the rippling flow of the draperies, how inevitably they bring to mind the native element, the home of the water people ! The Greek youths that ride along the Parthenon frieze, the wounded lionesses that roar defiance from the Assyrian bas-reliefs, the Japanese fish that swim in bronze, though cut off from their background or environment, yet again how perfectly each suggests its habitat through the magnifying imagination of the artist !

The combining imagination (the building up by additions which enhance and enliven) is just the reverse of the process we have been considering. It has to do with associations, with memories ; and the combination is brought about by images from hither and yon, that gather and join in the mind. There is some confusion just here between what is imagination in painting and what is mere composition, which Mr. Ruskin has tried to clear up by asserting that the former is intuitive and the latter is labored, that one works by genius and the other by laws and principles. But the distinction itself is somewhat labored, and in its practical working it seems to have small basis in reality. A gathering together of antique pavements, marble benches stained with iron rust, ideal figures clad in Greek garments, with various museum bric-a-brac illustrative of Greek life, such as we see in the pictures of Alma-Tadema, is certainly composition. It may be good or bad composition, it may be academic or naturalistic, it may have been put together laboriously, piece by piece, or flashed together by a momentary lightning of the mind; but, whatever the method or however brought about, one thing seems very certain, and that is, the work, in the hands of Alma-Tadema, contains not one spark of imagination. The same method of combining in the mind or working on the canvas with Delacroix or Turner or even J. S. Cotman would have almost certainly resulted in the imaginative.

It is a fond fancy of Mr. Ruskin, and also of ourselves, that genius despises laborious composition and does things with a sudden burst of inspiration. We think, because the completed work looks easy or reads easy, that it must have been done easily.

XIII.—VELASQUEZ, Innocent X.   Doria Gallery, Rome.

But the geniuses of the world have all put upon record their conviction that there is more virtue in perspiration than in inspiration. The great poets, whether in print or in paint, have spent their weeks and months—yes, years—composing, adjusting, putting in, and taking out. They have known what it was to "lick things into shape," to labor and be baffled, to despair and to hope anew. Goethe may have conceived "Faust" intuitively, but it took him something like fifty years to record his intuitions. He composed laboriously, and yet was no less a man of superlative imagination. Listen a moment to his Prologue to "Faust":

Raphael.

"The sun-orb sings in emulation
    Mid brother-spheres his ancient round:
His path predestined through creation
He ends with step of thunder-sound.
The angels from his visage splendid
Draw power, whose measure none can say;
The lofty works, uncomprehended,
Are bright as on the earliest day.

Gabriel.

" And swift, and swift beyond conceiving,
The splendor of the world goes round,
Day's Eden-brightness still relieving
The awful Night's intense profound:

The ocean-tides in foam are breaking,
Against the rocks deep bases hurled,
And both, the spheric race partaking,
Eternal, swift, are onward whirled!

Michael.

" And rival storms abroad are surging
From sea to land, from land to sea,
A chain of deepest action forging
Round all, in wrathful energy.
There flames a desolation, blazing
Before the Thunder's crashing way ;
Yet, Lord, thy messengers are praising
The gentle movement of thy Day." *

Here is the imagination presenting us with a great cosmic picture that in sublimity I venture to think has no superior in either poetry or painting ; yet it cannot be doubted that it was built up thought by thought, line upon line ; torn down perhaps a dozen times to be modelled anew with something added or omitted. In other words it has been composed, not flashed together by intuition.

The combining imagination in painting does not

---

* The original German lies open before me, but I prefer to give the quotation in a language which will not fail to be understood by all American readers. It is Bayard Taylor's translation, and so far as the imaginative conception is concerned it reproduces the original fairly well.

work differently from this. The picture is built up ; and memories often play a prominent part in the process. One may mingle lines from Greece with colors from Japan and an atmosphere from Holland if he will. The result might be something heterogeneous and incongruous, but it would nevertheless be a true enough display of the imagination. But such a gathering from hither and yon, such a mingling of many foreign elements, would not be necessary or essential or even usual in art. Pictures are made in simpler ways. Here, for example, is a sea-piece from the "Ancient Mariner," imagined and composed again, but brought together as a homogeneous whole.

> "The western wave was all aflame,
> The day was well-nigh done,
> Almost upon the western wave
> Rested the broad bright sun."

There the marine would seem to be quite complete, but Coleridge has yet to heighten the effect of the sunset by introducing a memory of an impression received perhaps in boyhood. His imagination, having conjured up the image of the phantom ship, combines it with the burning sunset :

> "When that strange shape drove suddenly
> Betwixt us and the sun."

> " And straight the sun was flecked with bars
>   (Heaven's Mother send us grace!)
>   As if through a dungeon grate he peered
>   With broad and burning face."

The introduction of the "dungeon grate" still further increases the effect. We now have the flaming sky, the sea, and the skeleton ship through which the sun mockingly peers, as through dungeon bars, at the dying crew. The effect is weird, uncanny, unearthly, just what Coleridge intended it should be. This, I should say, was the imagination adding and combining. And so far as I can see it is also the intelligent mind composing.

It would be difficult to find a parallel in painting to this picture from the "Ancient Mariner." One thinks at once of Turner's "Ulysses and Polyphemus" as resembling the Coleridge conception, because of the sea and the sun; but the likeness is superficial. In the Turner the spread of the sea, the golden waves in the foreground, the heave of the mountains out of the water, the spectral figure on the mountain top, the far distance of the ocean with the sun on the uttermost verge, are all highly imaginative; but the real glory of the picture is its decorative splendor rather than its expressive meaning. The "Fighting Téméraire," as we have already noted, is imaginative in the magnitude of the bulk and there is something of the Coleridge effect in the glare of the red setting sun that peers through clouds, taking its farewell look at the old war-ship being towed to its last berth ; but the imagination is not so clear-cut here as with Coleridge (Plate 11).

In some of Turner's Approaches to Venice there is perhaps a better example of the combining imagination, for Turner never hesitated about "composing" —putting things into the picture that were not there in reality ; and in the Venetian pictures he sometimes did this with startling results. I have in mind one of these pictures, where Venice is seen a mile or more away; but the domes of the Salute and the tops of the campaniles have been so shifted about to suit Turner's views of composition that I have never been able to determine whether the city is seen from the east or the west. And apparently Turner did not care anything about geography or topography. His imagination brought up out of the blue-green sea a city of palaces, builded of marble and hued like mother-of-pearl, with distant towers shining in the sun—a fairy city floating upon the sea, opalescent as a mirage, dream-like as an Eastern story, a glamour of mingled color and light beneath a vast-reaching sky glowing with the splendor of sun-shot clouds. It is most beautifully unreal, and yet by dint of its great imagination and suggestion it is more Venetian than Venice itself. It is that kind of distortion by the imagination which sacrifices the form to gain the spirit of things.

Here at Venice one can see the work of the combining imagination very well in some of the old Venetian pictures. Paolo Veronese, for instance, has upon the ceiling of one of the rooms in the Ducal Palace, a towering majestic figure, clad in silks and ermines, crowned with pearls and sceptred with power, seated under a gorgeous canopy in a chair of state, and representing the glory of Venice. She is a magnificent type of womanhood, splendid enough in herself to symbolize the splendor of Venice, but Paolo's imagination adds to her importance still further by placing her upon a portion of a great globe representing the world, while below at her feet are two superb figures representing Justice and Peace, offering the tributes of the sword and the olive branch (Plate 14).

Another Venetian, Tintoretto, had possibly more imagination than any other of his school—yes, any other Italian in art-history ; and yet it is not always possible to say just how his ideas originally took form. No doubt he labored and composed and tried effects by putting things in and taking them out. No doubt the " Ariadne and Bacchus," or the " Miracle of the Slave " (Plate 15) as we see it to-day, was the third or fourth thought instead of the first ; but there is no questioning the exaltation of the final

XIV.—PAOLO VERONESE, Venice Enthroned. Doge's Palace, Venice.

result. The subject of the Resurrection in his day had become a tradition in painting, and was usually shown as a square tomb of marble with a man rising from it between two angels. This stereotyped tradition had been handed down for centuries; but how greatly Tintoretto changed it and improved it in his picture in the Scuola San Rocco! He imagined the side of a mountain, a rock-cut tomb with angels pulling away the great door, and as it slowly opens the blinding light within the tomb bursts forth, and the figure of Christ rises swiftly, supported by the throbbing wings of angels.

However this last-named picture was produced, by combination or association, at least it is purely pictorial—that is, it deals with forms, lights, and colors, things that can be seen. I hardly know what to make of Mr. Ruskin's remarks upon some of the other pictures by Tintoretto, in the Scuola San Rocco. He seeks to exemplify the painter's ever-fertile imagination by pointing out, in the " Annunciation," that the corner-stone of the building is meant by Tintoretto to be that of the old Hebrew Dispensation, which has been retained by the builders as the corner-stone of the new Christian Dispensation ; and that, in the " Crucifixion," the donkey at the back eating the palm - branches recently thrown down before Christ upon his entry into Jerusalem is a great piece of imaginative sarcasm. I confess my inability to follow Mr. Ruskin just here, and I cannot believe that Tintoretto meant anything of the sort about either the corner-stone or the palm-branches. If he did, it was perhaps a mistake. The motives would be more literary than pictorial. I think it all exemplifies Mr. Ruskin's imagination rather than Tintoretto's, and in either case it has little to do with imagination in painting as generally understood among painters. Painting and the pictorial conception, it must be repeated, have to do with forms and colors seen by the eye or in the mind's eye ; they have very little to do with a sarcasm or a Hebraic mystery.

There is still another phase of imagination which figures in metaphysical text-books under the name of fancy. It is sometimes called the passive imagination, apparently for no reason other than distinction's sake. It is supposed to be temporary and accidental in its association of ideas and images, to be light, airy, capricious, perhaps indefinite ; whereas, imagination is said to be more sober, serious, single in purpose, seeking unity of effect. The illustrations usually cited are taken from Shakespeare. The "Midsummer Night's Dream" is said to be a product of fancy, while "Lear" or "Hamlet" is a work of the imagination. But again I must confess my inability to comprehend the distinction. The thought in the one case busies itself with a light or gay theme, and in the other with a sober or tragic theme ; but the mental process would seem to be the same in either case. The mind may grow happy over a birth or grieve over a death, but one mind and one imagination would seem flexible enough to comprehend them both. There is a difference in art between what is called the serious and what is called the clever ; but the imagination has nothing to do with it. A figure of a soubrette dashed off in a Parisian studio, and sent in a hurry to a Salon or Academy exhibition as a "stunning thing," may be clever. Mr. La Farge has defined such cleverness as "intelligence working for the moment without a background of previous thought or strong senti- ment." And this definition suggests that the seri- ous in art is just the opposite of the clever. A fig- ure by Millet, such as that of "The Sower," is serious just because the intelligence has been work- ing upon it for many months. But, in spite of call- ing a Jacquet soubrette fanciful and a Millet sower imaginative, there would seem to be no difference in the mental processes. The difference is one of sub- ject, time, men, original endowment ; not a differ- ence in the kind of thought.

The fantastic is also a product of the imagination, but it is a lighter, more volatile and irresponsible ex- pression than fancy. It is the imagination just es- caping from control, dominated by caprice and leaning toward the bizarre. The griffins and the spouting dragons along the gutters of the Gothic churches, and the boar-headed, bird-footed devils of early art are perhaps fair illustrations of it. In modern painting Blake and Monticelli came perilously near the fantastic in some of their creations. Turner in his last years quite lost himself in fantasy, and a number of the painters in France and England might be named as illustrating the tendency to the bizarre. When the bizarre is finally reached we may still recognize it as the working imagination, but uncontrolled by reason. Our dreams which often strike us as so absurd are good instances of the play of the imagination unfettered by reason ; and if our dreamland conceptions could be reduced to art we would undoubtedly have what we have called the bizarre. Caricature and the grotesque are different again. They are conscious distortions, designed exaggerations of certain features for effect. They are not ruled so much by either fancy or caprice as by a sensible view of the extravagant.

There is no metaphysical or æsthetic term to designate an absence of the imagination, but possibly the words "baroque" or "bombastic" will suggest the results in art. And there is no lack of material to illustrate it. Unfortunately the master minds in both poetry and painting have been few and far between. The names and works that have come down

XV —TINTORETTO, Miracle of Slave. Academy, Venice.

to us from the past are the survivals from many siftings ; and the few geniuses of the present are perhaps still obscured by the bombastic performances of smaller men.   The Robert Montgomerys and the Martin Farquhar Tuppers somehow contrive to make a stir and delude the public into considering them as great originals.   They have not imagination of their own, so they imitate the imaginative utterances and styles of others.   Not one but many styles of many men are thus brought together in a conglomeration that may deceive the groundlings into thinking it genuine poetry ; but the judicious soon find out its true character.   Of course, all imitators try to imitate the inimitable individualities.   The Montgomerys and the Tuppers aspire to no less than Shakespeare and Milton.   Just so in pictorial art. Vasari, Guido, the Caracci reached out for the imaginations of Michael Angelo, Raphael, and Correggio. The result was the contorted bombastic art of the Decadence than which nothing could be less imaginative and more monstrous.   The mind of a Michael Angelo of necessity distorted the image in the first place and then a Salviati came along to distort the distortion!   The figure of a Madonna, for instance, is elongated by Correggio for grace, and Parmigianino following after elongated the elongation !   This is what I have called the bombastic.   It is indicative of a lack of imagination.   Modern painting is full of it. The attempts at the heroic that overstep the sublime and fall into the ridiculous, the rant and high-sounding utterances of the brush, the inflated figures of allegory and the vacuous types of symbolism, are all illustrative of it.

But the bombastic and its companion evils in art need no further consideration at this time. It is not my aim to illustrate the deficiencies of painting, but to point out its higher beauties, and if the reverse of the shield is occasionally shown it is but to illustrate and emphasize the brighter side. Perhaps one may be pardoned for thinking that sometimes the analysis of error is a potent factor in the establishment of truth.

CHAPTER IV

PICTORIAL POETRY

TIME was, and not very long ago at that, when an argument for poetic thought in art would have been considered superfluous. Everyone was agreed that the higher aim of language was to convey an idea, a feeling, or an emotion. That the language should be beautiful in itself was an advantage, but there was never any doubt that the thought expressed was greater than the manner of its expression. To-day it would seem that we have changed all that. The moderns are insisting that language is language for its own sake, and art is art for art's sake. They are, to a certain extent, right in their contention ; for there is great beauty in methods, materials and the general decorative appearance.* But perhaps they insist too much. We are not yet prepared to admit that because Tennyson's poetry sounds well, his thoughts have no value ; nor, for all Tintoretto's fine form

* I have stated the case for the decorative side and for the technical beauties of painting in *Art for Art's Sake*, New York, 1902.

and color, can we believe his poetic imagination a wholly unnecessary factor in his art.

The technical and the decorative beauties of painting, however important they may be, are not necessarily the final aim of the picture. In the hands of all the great painters of the world they have been only a means to an end. The Michael Angelos, the Rembrandts, the Raphaels, and the Titians have generally had an ulterior meaning in their work. And by "meaning" I do not mean anything very abstruse or metaphysical, nor am I thinking of anything ethical, allegorical, or anecdotal. The idea which a picture may contain is not necessarily one that points a moral, nor need it have anything to do with heroic action or romantic sentiment or fictional occurrence. There are many ideas, noble in themselves, that find expression in literature better than in painting, and it is a sound rule in all the arts that a conception which can be well told in one art has no excuse for being badly told in another art. The materials and their application to the best advantage are always to be regarded. Why waste effort in cutting glass when you can blow it ? Why chisel curtains in marble when you can weave them in cloth? Why tell sequential stories, moral, narrative, or historical, in paint when it can be done more easily in writing ? And why describe landscapes in writing when you can do it so much better in painting ? It

XVI.—DAUB:GNY, Spring. Louvre, Paris.

is mere consumption of energy and distortion of materials to write down the colors of the sunset or to paint the history of Greece or Rome.

It is well for us then at the start that we have no misunderstanding about the relationship between literature and art. That they are related in measure may be said with equal truth of preaching and science, of poetry and politics, of music and history. Science has been preached and politics have been poetized, and history has been shrieked in a high treble at the opera. Just so art has illustrated literature and literature art; but it can hardly be contended that any one of them has been put to its proper purpose. The main affair of literature is to illustrate literature, and the business of art is primarily to produce art. They are independent pursuits and there is no need of confounding their aims or being confused by their apparent resemblances.

Therefore, in using the phrase pictorial poetry I would be understood as meaning *pictorial* poetry and not *literary* poetry. They are two quite different things by virtue of their means of expression. The idea in art, whether poetic or otherwise, has its material limitations, which we must not fail to take into account. The first limitation is the major one and it demands that painting deal with things *seen*. We have referred to this in speaking of Tintoretto's

" Annunciation," but it is worth while to take it up again and more definitely.

The couplet,

> " The mind that broods o'er guilty woes
> Is like the scorpion girt by fire,"

is certainly a poetic image ; but fancy, if you can, how a painter would paint that brooding mind. He could not do it. Why? Because it is not tangible, it cannot be seen, it has no form or color. It is an abstract idea to be comprehended by the mind through sound, and belongs to literature. Perhaps you think the painter might have rendered it by showing a sad face and a wrinkled brow, but how would you know whether the wrinkles came from mental or from physical pain? And what can he say to you about " guilty woes" with a paint brush? The writer can tell you about the inside and the outside of the head, but the painter is limited to the outside.

The inability of painting to deal with sound—a something without tangible form—may be further illustrated by Millet's celebrated picture of the " Angelus." It has already served me for illustration, but I shall not at this time go out of my way for a newer example. The expressed thought of the picture, the whole story, hinges on the sound of a church-bell— the Angelus bell of sunset. How does Millet attempt to picture this sound ? Why, by painting far back

in the distance a church-spire seen against a sunset
sky, and in the foreground two peasants with bowed
heads. But the effort at sound is inadequate. The
peal of the bell is beyond the reach of paints and
brushes. The most brilliant colors make no sound.
It is not to be wondered at, therefore, that there have
been half a dozen different readings of the picture's
meaning. The idea of the Angelus is in the picture
only because it has been read into it by the title of
the work. That is a leaning upon literature which
is unnecessary in art. The painting should require
no explanation by language.

It need not be denied that the Angelus story is
poetic ; but it is perfectly just and proper to contend
that by its dependence upon sound it is better fitted
for literature than for art. A Tennyson could have
made a poem about it wherein the sound of the bells
would have been in the cadences of the language—in
the very syllables breaking upon the ear. We all
remember his flying notes from the horns of Elfland
in "The Princess."

> " Oh hark, oh hear ! how thin and clear
>   And thinner, clearer, further going.
> Ah ! sweet and far, from cliff and scar,
>   The horns of Elfland faintly blowing."

In those lines we have the idea of sound conveyed
to us most forcibly. The flow of the words describes

exactly (and they even imitate) the long travel of the bugle notes, far across the lake, up the vales, and finally dying away into the remotest distance. Surely the thought of that passage is best told in language. What could pigments do with it? What could a fine technician like Bargue or a poet in paint like Delacroix make of that mellow music ? They might picture someone with a horn to his lips and a mountain lake in the background ; but the fetching part of those Elfland horns is not their *look*, but their *sound*. What could the painters do with the sound ? Why nothing except to let it alone. A flat canvas will not discourse music like the board of a piano. Forms and colors may talk very eloquently to the eye, but they say nothing to the ear. The old division of the arts made over a century ago by Lessing is still acceptable to-day. The fine arts of architecture, sculpture, and painting address the sense of sight ; the fine arts of music and literature address the sense of hearing. Therefore, let us assume that such thoughts, ideas, or emotions, poetic or otherwise, as a painter may wish to express in painting should be primarily pictorial by addressing the sense of sight.

There is another, a minor limitation put upon painting which in its way is quite as binding as the major one. This is the time limit. A painting is not a shifting panorama like a drama. It cannot picture

XVII.—BENOZZO GOZZOLI, Adoration of Kings (detail). Riccardi Palace. Florence.

(though it may hint at) the past or the future; it can deal adequately only with the present. You may turn the leaves of a book and pass from Greek days to the present time as you read; but you cannot do that with a picture. It does not turn or shift or show any more than the one face. Therefore the idea in art, generally speaking, should not concern itself with time, or be dependent upon shiftings of scene, or deal with anything that has gone before or is to come after. A picture of Charlotte Corday on the way to the guillotine indicates a present happening, and, so far as it offers something complete in itself, it is pictorial enough; but the picture fails to tell us that some days before she assassinated Marat, and that some minutes later she herself will be done away with by the executioner's knife. The title of the picture may tell us her story, but then that is leaning upon literature again. A painting of "Alexander Entering Babylon" by Lebrun may show us marching troops, elephants, chariots, and Alexander himself surrounded by his generals. It is a present scene; but how shall the picture tell you who Alexander was, what battles he fought, what ending he came to? It may suggest the past and the future by the present condition, but the suggestion is often too vague for human comprehension. Time-movement, sequential events are really beyond the reach of pigments.

It is much easier deciding what painting can picture than what it cannot.   We have only to ask ourselves if the subject is one that may be comprehended by the unaided eye, and if it is a theme
completed in present time.   Painting moves freely
only within these boundaries, whereas literature moves
within and without them as it pleases, and with meas-
urable success even in pictorial themes.   Here is a
word-landscape by Scott that illustrates my meaning :

> " Sweet Teviot, on thy silver tide
>   The glaring bale-fires blaze no more,
> No longer steel-clad warriors ride
>   Along thy wild and willowed shore."

There we have a picture painted in words.   Scott
has gone poaching into the domain of pictorial art,
and with astonishing results.   It is a picture.   Literature is certainly capable of dealing with forms
and colors as with abstractions of the mind, but it
cannot handle them so well, perhaps, as painting.
We have here not abstractions, but entities of form
and color.   There is something for the painter to
grasp with pencil and brush.   Perhaps he can paint
the "silver tide " and the " willowed shore " more
effectively than Scott can describe them ; and if he
should paint them with that feeling which would
give us the wildness of the shore, the weirdness of
the bale-fires, the crush and rush of steel-clad war-

riors along the banks, paralleling the push-forward of the stream itself, we should have what I am disposed to call pictorial poetry.

But, if you please, it is not to be inferred that this pictorial poetry is to be gotten out of literary poetry only. Painting is no mere servant of literature, whose duty it is to illustrate rather than create. There is no reason why the painter, looking at the river Teviot, should not see poetry in it as well as the writer. Delacroix not only could but did see it. Turner saw the same kind of romantic sentiment as Scott in all the rivers he ever pictured. Daubigny saw it less romantically, but with more of the real charm of nature, along the banks of the Marne ; and Claude Monet has certainly shown us many times the poetry of light, color, and rushing, dancing water on the Seine. Monet is just as susceptible to poetic impressions as Leconte de Lisle, only his poetry comes to him in forms and colors rather than in the measured cadences of language. It is painter's poetry, not writer's poetry.

It is true enough that painting has often taken its themes from the play, the novel, and the poem, and not without success. All the older painters of England spent their time illustrating Shakespeare and Milton. But it was not at all necessary, nor did it result in the best kind of art. And as for literature taking its theme from painting, one can pick illus-

trations of it in quantity from any anthology.   For
instance, what is more probable than that Scott was
looking at a painting when writing this :

> " No earthly flame blazed e'er so bright
>   It shone like heaven's own blessed light,
>   And, issuing from the tomb,
>   Showed the monk's cowl and visage pale,
>   Danced on the dark-browed warrior's mail,
>   And kissed his waving plume."

The light-and-shade of the scene seems to bring to
mind some lost Correggio. And how like Giorgione is the "flame" dancing on the warrior's mail,
and "kissing his waving plume!" (Plate 24.) In
reading the "Faery Queene" one finds a whole gallery of pictures painted with words. Spenser would
have made a painter, for he had the pictorial mind.
Milton is not unlike him; and Shakespeare goes
hither and yon over all fields and through all departments. Here, for example, is his *genre* picture of
the hounds of Theseus :

> " My hounds are bred out of the Spartan kind,
>   So flewed, so sanded : and their heads are hung
>   With ears that sweep away the morning dew ;
>   Crook-kneed and dew-lapp'd like Thessalian bulls."

Surely a very striking picture, but after all you cannot see Shakespeare's hounds so completely and perfectly as those of Velasquez or Snyders or Troyon.

XVIII.—VAN DYCK, Jean Grusset Richardot. Louvre, Paris.

Sculpture, too, may furnish material for good poetry, as witness this description of the marble figures upon the tomb in the Church of Brou.

" So rest, forever rest, O princely Pair !
    In your high church 'mid the still mountain air,
    Where horn and hound and vassals never come.
    Only the blessed saints are smiling dumb
    From the rich painted windows of the nave
    On aisle and transept and your marble grave ;

. . . .

    So sleep, forever sleep, O marble Pair !
    Or if ye wake, let it be then, when fair
    On the carved western front a flood of light
    Streams from the setting sun, and colors bright
    Prophets, transfigured Saints and Martyrs brave,
    In the vast western window of the nave ;
    And on the pavement round the tomb there glints
    A chequer-work of glowing sapphire tints
    And amethyst and ruby. . . ."

Matthew Arnold has certainly made a striking picture in words out of the tomb and its figures, but again the poetry is plastic—that is, fitted for sculpture or painting.

So it is—to repeat and summarize—that the writer with his words shows things picturesque and sculpturesque—inadequately perhaps as compared with the plastic mediums, but nevertheless effectively ; but not so the painter with his colors. The brush will not reveal and can scarcely do more than hint at things without form. It is perhaps possible for painting to be as clear-cut and as definite in its ideas as literature, but, as a matter of fact, it seldom is so. More often there is suggestion than realization, and the poetry comes to us in an almost indescribable feeling or sentiment of the painter. Indeed, the greater part of what we have called "pictorial po-etry" lies in a glimmering consciousness of beauty, an impression that charms, a feeling that sways, rather than in any exact statement.

Now that word "feeling" is not a cant expression of dilettanteism. It has a distinct meaning in all the arts. In the presence of beauty the artist "feels" that beauty and is emotionally moved by it as you or I might be moved by an heroic action, a splendid sunset, or a fine burst of orchestral music. He responds to the charm and yet is not able to ex-press his whole feeling, not even in words, much less in forms and colors. With all the resources of lan-guage and with all his skill in expression Tennyson is not cunning enough to tell the whole passionate tale of Arthur and Launcelot and Guinevere—the three who lived and loved and died so many years ago and now lie "low in the dust of half-forgotten kings." All the heroism, the nobility, the splendid pathos of those lives, could not be put into words. Tennyson could only summon up a sentiment about them, and deeply imbued with that sentiment, he left a tinge of unutterable sadness in the poem which you and I feel and love, and yet can but poorly describe. We do not know it like a mathematical problem ; we *feel* it.

And consider that old man forsaken of his children —Lear. His complaints and tempers seem almost childish at times ; and yet through that play, more than through any other written expression of human woe, runs the feeling and the passion of a great heart breaking through ingratitude. Again think of that last act in "The Cenci," with Beatrice cursed by fate, stained with crime, and finally brought face to face with trial and death. Have you ever read or known of such another whirlwind of wildness and calmness, of weakness and fortitude, of courage and fear ! And the ghastly, creeping horror of it all ! Can you not feel it? Neither Shakespeare nor Shelley can chart and scale upon a board the passion he would show us. It could not be pinned down or summed up scientifically. It can, in fact, be brought home to us only by that great under-current running through all notable art—feeling.

Consider once again Wagner's "Götterdämmerung !" How would it be possible to tell with musical notes all the tragic power that lies in that opera ? Wagner himself was not able to do it. What he did was to summon up a romantic mood of mind by contemplating the theme in his imagination and then, to suggest by a choice of motives and orchestration, the immense passion of the story. By following the orchestration rather than the individual singers you can feel in the different *motifs* the poetry of that heroic age—the glorious achievements, the sad passing, the mournful sunset, the fading into oblivion of those who ruled the beautiful world. If you cannot feel the mystery, the sadness, the splendor of it all, I am afraid it argues some want of music and romance in your soul rather than a want of poetry in the opera. The feeling is there; it is the last thing perhaps to be recognized by the student of music, and yet it is the one thing above all others that has made Wagner a great poet. He could suggest more than he could describe, and because he suggests and does not describe is one reason why he is, at first, so difficult to understand.

The picture in this respect, is not different from music or literary poetry. Poetic feeling in painting may be and has been shown in many subjects and in many ways. If we go back to the Gothic period in Italy, when the painters were just emerging from mediævalism, we shall find a profound feeling for religion. It shows in Giotto and the Florentines, in Duccio and the Sienese. They do not know how to draw, color, or light a picture correctly; they are just learning to paint, and like children they feel in-

XIX.—GAINSBOROUGH, Mrs. Siddons.   National Gallery, London.

finitely more than they can express. And they do not try to express any precise or detailed account of Christianity. They could not if they would. That which is called "religious feeling" in the altar-pieces of the Gothic period and the early Renaissance is really a mental and emotional attitude of the painter —a fine sentiment, an exquisite tenderness in the presentation of biblical themes and characters. It is no matter whether the sentiment is really religious or merely human; it is in either case poetic. And it is no matter whether the painter's devotion and earnestness were misplaced or not; at least they were sincere. There never was a time in the history of painting when the body of artists believed more thoroughly in their theme, their work, and themselves than during that early Italian time.

You can see this well exemplified in Orcagna—in his "Last Judgment" in Santa Maria Novella. The Madonna looking up at her Son is an embodiment of all the pietistic sentiment of the time. The figure is ill-drawn, stiff, archaic-looking; but in the white-cowled face what purity, what serenity, what pathos! The clasped hands seem moved in prayer; the up-turned eyes look unutterable adoration. Orcagna is bent upon telling the faith of the Madonna in her Son, but he can only do so by telling the faith that is within his own soul. His revelation is a self-revelation, but it is not the less a religious feeling and a poetic feeling. Is this not equally true of that pious monk of San Marco, Fra Angelico ? Can there be any doubt about his life-long sympathy with religion and the religious theme in art ? It was his sympathy that begat his painting. That sweet, fair face full of divine tenderness, which we have so often seen in the copies of his trumpet-blowing angels, is it not the earthly embodiment of a divine spirit ?

Fra Angelico was the last of the great religionists in art, and before his death the sentiment of religion began to wane in the works of his contemporaries. They were straying from the religious to the naturalistic subject, but wherever their sympathy extended their feeling showed. When Masaccio, Benozzo, Botticelli, and Leonardo began to study the outer world with what earnestness and love they pictured the humanity, the trees, the grasses, the flowers, the long, flowing hill-lines, and the wide, expanding Italian sky. Botticelli's "Allegory of Spring" (Plate 29) or Benozzo's "Adoration of the Magi" in the Riccardi palace (Plates 2 and 17) or Leonardo's face of "Mona Lisa" must have been seen sympathetically and thought over passionately, else we never should have felt their beauty. Benozzo, inheriting his religious point of view from Fra Angelico, blends his love of man, animals, and landscape with his belief that they are all made for righteousness ; Botticelli is so intense that he is half-morbid in his sensitiveness ; and Leonardo, with that charm of mood and sweetness of disposition in the "Mona Lisa," is really transcendental. It is all fine, pictorial poetry, howbeit more in the suggestion than in the absolute realization.

This quality of poetry shown so largely in what I have called "feeling" is apparent in all great art, regardless of nationality or subject. The Venetians, for example, had none of the intense piety of the Umbrians, but they had perhaps just as much poetry. Even the early Venetians, like Carpaccio and Bellini, were more material than Fra Angelico and Filippino. They painted the Madonna with all seriousness and sincerity, with belief in the truth of their theme, but with a human side, as noble in its way as the spiritual, and just as truly marked by poetic feeling (Plate 7). After them came another painter, of greater skill and power. He was not so boyish in his enthusiasm as Carpaccio, but Theocritus in love with pastoral nature never had so much feeling for the pure joy of living as Giorgione. His shepherds seated on a hill-side playing and singing, in a fine landscape and under a blue sky, make up a picture far removed in spirit from theology, philosophy, science, war, or commerce. The world of action is forgotten and in its place there is Arcadia with sunlight and flowers, with beautiful women and strong men. But is it not nobly poetic ? When

Giorgione painted the Castelfranco Madonna (Plate 24) he did not change his spirit to suit the subject. The picture has written upon the face of the Madonna as upon the face of the landscape : "I believe in the beauty and glory of the world." You may call this a pagan belief if you choose, but it is with Giorgione a sincere and a poetic belief.

Correggio at Parma was not materially different from Giorgione as regards the spirit of his art. His religious characters were only so in name. He never had the slightest sympathy with the melodramatic side of the Christian faith and could not depict the tragic without becoming repulsive ; but he saw the beauty of women and children in landscape and he felt the splendor of sunlight and shadow and color (Plate 8). There is no mystery or austerity or solemnity or intellectuality about his characters. They are not burdened with the cares of the world ; but how serenely and superbly they move and have their being ! What grace of action ! What poetry of motion ! What loveliness of color ! Shall you say that there is no poetry in that which appeals directly to the senses, that which belongs only to the earth ? As well contend that there is no beauty in the blue sky, no loveliness in flowers, no grace in the wave that curves and falls on the beach.

If we move to the north, passing the splendid achievements of Titian, Tintoretto, Palma, and

XX.—GÉRÔME, Napoleon before the Sphinx.

Paolo Veronese, passing the mysticism of Dürer and the intense humanity of Holbein, passing the radiant splendor of Rubens and the courtly elegance of Van Dyck, we shall come eventually to Holland and to those Dutchmen whom the academicians declared had no style. There we shall find the arch-heretic, Rembrandt, who had nothing of Greek form and academic composition, and yet possessed what was worth far more—deep human feeling. His characters are only poor Dutch peasants; his Christ is a forlorn, bare-footed, frail-bodied outcast; his backgrounds are generally squalid, ill-lighted interiors. There is no splendor of architecture, no glamour of wealth, no fair Italian valley with a deep-blue sky above it. His materials for making the pictorial poem were slight enough; but never a picture was painted with so much poetic pathos as that little "Supper at Emmaus" in the Louvre. The intense sympathy of Rembrandt going out to the poor and oppressed all his life, went out above all others to that One who was poor and despised—the lowly One who taught the gospel of love. No one can look upon any of the peasants of Rembrandt without being conscious of the man's deep feeling. His *technique*, of course, is marvellous; but so is his insight and his capacity to feel. If it were not so we should gain little pleasure from his subjects.

Have you never wondered what it is in art that

makes a painter's interpretation of a scene more agreeable than the scene itself? If you had a few sheep, a French peasant, a straw-thatched cottage, and a barren plain you would have the materials for a Millet picture. Suppose you lived in a fine country place, how long would the cottage stand near you before you had it torn down, or the shepherd and sheep roam your lawns before you had them driven off by dogs? You would not care for them, they would not be beautiful, they would not even be interesting after the first day. Why is it then that you pay thousands of dollars for a picture of the shepherd and his sheep to hang in your drawing-room, when you would not have the originals within gun-shot? Is it not that the materials have something added to them? Are they not helped in their representation by the painter's insight and his capacity to feel?

Rembrandt saw a deeper meaning in his commonplace materials than you or I. He saw that under the tattered gaberdine of the Amsterdam Jew beat the heart and throbbed the brain of all humanity. The Jew was typical of universal suffering—an epitome of humanity, and at the same time an exemplar of inhumanity. And think you there is no force, no nobility in the uncouth, heavy-set peasant of Holland? Can you not see the stamp of character in the deep-marked face and the labor-worn form?

Can you not see that the man is self-made, made strong by hardships; that he has been developed and brought to maturity through adversity? It is this beauty of character that Rembrandt is bringing to your notice. And can you believe that there is no charm in the low-lying land of the Dutchman—the land where clouds roll out to sea by day, and fogs drift inland by night? Can you not see that here, too, is something developed through adversity, that this domain has been wrested from the sea and turned into flower - spattered meadows, fields of grain, ranks of polders, groves of trees? Have not man and country a peculiar beauty of their own—a beauty of character?

And how different is it with the peasantry of France? These gleaners in the fields as they bend forward to gather the stray stalks, how fine they are in their great simple outlines, how substantial in body, how excellent in motion (Plate 4)! And see how they harmonize with the coloring of the stubble and fit into their atmospheric place, so that they are of a piece with the foreground, background, and sky—cemented, blended into one, by the warm haze of a July afternoon. Is then this flat space of stubble under the burning summer sun, this bare treeless field, "La belle France" which every Frenchman and many a foreigner raves about? Yes; only doubly intensified. This is the substance and the solidity of France—the yielding, arable soil that makes the wealth of France. And this sower moving silently in the shadow of the hill, moving with such rhythmic motion, tired and worn yet swinging and sowing—the sun gone down and twilight upon him, yet still without a murmur, without a falter, swinging and sowing the grain—is this the brave Frenchman whose kith and kin fought at Marengo and Waterloo ? Yes; only doubly intensified. He is the brawn and muscle of France—the original producer, the planter and sustainer of the race. Has he, who has so labored, so wrestled with stubborn circumstance and wrought success from meagre opportunity, has he not a character of his own that may be called beautiful in art ? And the land he has broken and made so productive, the soil that he sprang from and is so intimately associated with, has it not a character of landscape peculiarly its own and again pictorially beautiful ?

Millet and Rembrandt knew this truth of character in both man and nature, and often they must have thrown down their brushes in despair of ever telling it; but knowing it so well and feeling it so deeply, they could not choose but leave the mark of their feeling in their pictures. And they produced great democratic art—the assertion that all beauty does not lie in the straight nose, the Apollo mouth, and the Apoxyomenos form ; and that poetry

XXI.—MICHAEL ANGELO, Delphic Sibyl. Sistine Chapel, Rome.

is not alone the tale of classic heroes and mediæval marauders. The man, though rag-patched, may be a king ; the land, though no Arcadian grove, is still the great productive mother-earth. Shall we have an aristocracy solely of wealth, or an aristocracy solely of birth ? May there not also be an aristocracy of character ?

I have said that this poetic feeling in art found its way into many subjects. The examples given are but a handful from that vast world of life from which the painter is privileged to draw ; and you must not infer that it has to do with religion and the pathos of humble life alone. Corot, for instance, never painted anything that expressed either. His was the poetry of light (Plate 9) as Rousseau's the poetry of the forest and Daubigny's the poetry of the meadow and the river-bank (Plate 16). And are there not pæans of beauty unmixed in the voyaging clouds of Constable, the serene blue skies of Courbet, the silvery mists of Maris, the stormy coasts of Winslow Homer ? A portrait by Gainsborough (Plate 19) or Van Dyck (Plate 18), an interior by Van der Meer of Delft or Pieter de Hooge, a Venetian scene by Guardi or Bunce, a battle or shipwreck by Delacroix, a tiger and a serpent by Barye, may any or all of them be poetic. The poetry is in the man, not the subject. Whatever the poet sees, if it appeals to him emotionally, may start that train of feeling which evitably creeps into the canvas—creeps in just as when one is in a gay or sad mood his gayety or sadness will tinge the current of his playing or his singing or be apparent in his conversation.

Again let me repeat that the thought in pictures, whether poetic or otherwise, is seldom so definite or precise as in literature. Meissonier in his "Napoleon in 1814" wishes to tell you of the Emperor's defeat, but the only way he can do it is to paint a man on horseback alone on the brow of a hill with a gloomy, set face and a dark sky. It is suggestion rather than realization. Gérôme is one of the best story-tellers with the paint-brush of the present times, but what does he mean by his "Napoleon before the Sphinx" (Plate 20)? Evidently a contrast has been thought of—a contrast between the tiny figure on horseback and the colossal head looming above the desert sands—but what precisely does the contrast mean? Is this the modern world against the whole vast past? Is it France, the latest of nations, conquering Egypt, the earliest of nations? Or is this little man on horseback the intellectual force, the Œdipus of the West, come at last to Egypt to solve the riddle of the Sphinx? You see the actual thought is not so accurately read. Again, I am disposed to think that in Mr. Watts's "Love and Death" the little god upon the doorstep falling back among the flowers before the great out-

stretched arm of Death means that into every house
where love and joy and flowers have been supreme,
the spectre of death must sooner or later enter.
But I do not know that Mr. Watts had quite that
idea when he painted the picture. It is because the
thought in painting is always more or less indefinite
as compared with literature that so many different
meanings are read into or out of celebrated pictures.
Art-critics and historians are still explaining Titian's
"Venus Equipping Cupid" and Botticelli's "Allegory of Spring." Pictorial language is not like the
vernacular of speech ; it is not even written so that
all alike may comprehend its spirit. At best it is
a sign language that permits of varying interpreta-
tions, and it is not by any means the best medium of
conveying abstract ideas from one mind to another.
But like music it is very responsive to emotional feeling and conveys the poetic mood or sentiment,
sometimes with great force.

Indeed, true pictorial feeling finds its way into still
less clear conceptions than we have cited. The very
means of expression are often tinged by it. There
may be no deep sentiment in the subject or characters. It may be only a group of tavern brawlers by
Jan Steen or a smirking fish-wife by Frans Hals,
and yet the picture may be handled in color and
light with such charm as to produce a prismatic
poem. Diaz could and did paint flowers as worthy

of Paradise as Ghiberti's "Gates of the Baptistery," solely because of his fine feeling for color. Sometimes there is a feeling for the sweep and flow of lines, as in Raphael, Tintoretto, and Rubens, that is poetic in the best sense of the word, and in Delacroix's colors there is often the haunting suggestion of passion, fury, fire, and death. The subject may count for little. What the painter feels about it may make it poetic. Decamp got poetry out of the exact value of a spot of sunshine falling on the floor ; and Chardin found it in the textures of pots and pans in a kitchen.

Paint itself may be made poetic by the sympathetic handling of it, just as words and sentences in literature. There is nothing remarkably poetic in thought about Byron's

"Before St. Mark's still glow his steeds of brass,
    Their gilded collars glittering in the sun,"

but can you not feel in the expression of it the stately and majestic march of numbers ? You may think there is nothing remarkable in thought in the flying figures of William Blake. They are descriptions like Byron's couplet, but under them is the feeling of vast sweeping power. This is all poetry of a most sovereign kind ; and that, too, shown in the means of expression—in the *technique* of art. The same kind of feeling appears in the contours of Leonardo, in the light-and-shade of Correggio, in the coloring of Paolo Veronese, in the modelling of Velasquez, in the brush-work of Manet. It rises to the sublime with Michael Angelo ; it abides in the smallest things of earth in the hands of the Japanese. Into the infinitely little as into the infinitely great the feeling of the man may infuse that true poetry of painting which is perhaps the highest as it is the ultimate aim of pictorial art. That it is not the only aim we shall see immediately when we come to discuss the decorative value of painting.

CHAPTER V

THE DECORATIVE QUALITY

WE could easily settle, *ex cathedra,* this matter of art if our views were the only ones to be considered ; but, unfortunately, intelligent people differ with us, and the painter himself is often our most determined antagonist. The painter, in fact, has opinions of his own about his pictures and he sometimes asserts them with no uncertain voice. His most persistent assertion is that the picture should be something decorative in form or color—be something beautiful to look at—rather than something moral, intellectual, or narrative. But the public, being differently minded, keeps insisting that the picture should be something in subject or have some literary meaning ; and, consequently, it often misses the decorative altogether. So it is that there is plenty of material for disagreement. The painter and his public seem ever at swords' points. Let us to-day review the case for the plaintiff and to-morrow perhaps we can sum up for the defendant public.

It is true, to begin with, that the average person who takes an interest in painting and attends gallery

exhibitions often shoots wide of the mark in his ap-
preciations.   He starts wrong by devoting too much
attention to pictures that have pretty faces and tell
pretty stories.   He is over-fond of heroes and hero-
ines, plots and tales, dramatic scenes from history, or
familiar characters in fiction.   The ideal, whether in
figure, face or landscape, pleases him ; and he does
not object to a laugh over the comic or the ludicrous.
But he cannot abide coarse peasants or fishermen in
art ; Dutch pictures with their tavern brawls are not
to his taste ; and he persists in misunderstanding Italian people dressed in modern garb and representing
sacred characters.   Anachronisms of type, furniture,
architecture, bother him beyond measure.   The Madonna and the Apostles were Jews and lived in
Judea, and he wishes an archæological report of the
race, country, climate and soil.   Of course, he does
not care for portraits by Velasquez with their out-
landish dresses, or large Flemish women by Rubens,
or the "splashy" painting of Dutch burghers by
Frans Hals.   In short the average person is devoted
to the pleasant subject in art and is continually asking of the picture : What does it mean ?

The view of the painter is very different from all
this.   He is not interested in the pretty face.   The
Madonnas and Saints whether Dutch, French, German, or Italian, do not interest him as Madonnas and
Saints.   A figure, whether sacred or profane, is to

him only a figure. As for the pretty story, the ideal,
the correct costume, he usually turns up his nose at
them. He is not always interested in what a picture
means. Too often perhaps he cares not a rap whether
it means anything or not. His question is first of
all : What does it look ? He wishes to know whether
that figure is well drawn, rightly placed, beautiful as
form solely and simply. Costume, whether right or
wrong, is no great matter ; but does that Madonna's
robe make for graceful line, or play well as a spot of
color ? The interior of a room has no significance
architecturally. It may be false to history ; but does
it make a good setting for the figures, does it lend
readily to light-and-shade, has it atmosphere (Plate
27) ? Finally, what is the result of the workmanship as a whole ? Has the painter handled his materials artistically, has he drawn his figures effectively,
has he arranged them compactly, has he brought his
lights-and-shades together truthfully, and has he
fused his color-masses harmoniously ? If so he has
produced a work of art, whether its subject means
much or means little.

The distinction which I would make is the old one
between art as representation and art as decoration.
The Arabic numeral 8, for example, conveys an abstract idea to the mind ; but if you draw a series of
linked 8's thus : 888888888888888888 you will have
something that conveys no idea and yet *looks* to the

XXII.—HALS, The Jolly Man. Rijks Museum, Amsterdam.

eye very like a graceful pattern for an architectural
frieze. The art which the "average person" seeks
in a picture-gallery represents an idea and has an
expressive meaning, the art which the painter
seeks in a gallery *looks* something and has a decorative meaning. It need not be inferred that the
two kinds of art are incompatible with each other.
On the contrary, they are closely united, for great
art is both expressive and decorative, and all art
is more or less decorative even when not expressive. Nor is it necessary to say that one is better
than the other. Perhaps it is the thing said rather
than the manner of saying that counts most with
us ; but what I wish to insist upon just here is that
the painter is first of all devoted to the manner of
saying, he is devoted to the decorative. We look at
his pictures and think how long he toiled over that
conception, how he walked the town, like Raphael,
searching for that pretty face, how he must have
studied to verify all his archæological facts. But,
no. His greatest effort has perhaps gone out in the
endeavor to make his tones harmonize, to get his
drawing right, to hold his picture together in its
planes, and make it one united impression of beautiful form and color.

You perhaps fancy that this contention for the
decorative on the part of the painter is some fad of
modernity. If you have that idea pray dismiss it, for

it has no basis in fact. The decorative sense goes back to the dawn of history. It was the very first sign of the art instinct in Primitive Man. Just how it originally came to the surface would be difficult to determine. Years ago Schiller put forth a theory which has been accepted by Mr. Herbert Spencer and others to the effect that it arose through the play-impulse ; and that art in its early significance was merely the result of man's superfluous energy— something done for pleasure in an idle hour. That is to say, the Stone Age man ornamented his weapons of the chase and his domestic utensils with color and line because he had too great a supply of animal spirits. And the safety valve where his spirits blew off was art ! We are to infer then that the decorative came into existence through man's delight in form and color and because he had nothing better to do. The theory is ingenious but not wholly convincing. It is quite as reasonable to argue with Mr. Whistler that when the so-called Primitive Man set out for the chase in the morning there was some weak or crippled brother of the tribe who had not enough animal spirits to join the band, and was left behind with the women to do camp work. He could not draw bow or fight and so it is possible that he was put to work at making weapons, carving implements, moulding, decorating, and baking pottery. He was at first no doubt an awkward workman ; but as his hands became more deft and his senses more acute he rounded shapes and forms with growing grace, and put patterns upon bowls and knife-handles with more justness of balance and appropriateness of design.

It is interesting to observe that almost at the start this primitive artist recognized the problem of adapting design and color to a given space—a problem that is to-day continually up for solution in every studio in the country. He recognized that the body of an ordinary vase, for instance, was capable of receiving one sort of a design—an open, free pattern perhaps,—the neck of it required something like a narrow-band pattern, the top or cover required a circular pattern. It was not long before our primitive artist found that the secret of good decoration lay in filling given spaces symmetrically ; and that the sense of order, harmony, and proportion were necessities of his craft. He found the same problem staring him in the face when he left his pottery and its geometrical designs and began scratching the outlines of animals and men upon weapons or flat surfaces of stone. He had to adapt his figures to his space— adapt them rhythmically, decoratively. If the space happened to be a dagger-handle then the figures were necessarily of diminutive size or represented in horizontal attitudes ; if the space were a shield then the figures had to carry the action around the centre in rows perhaps ; if it were an upright panel of clay or stone then the figures were required to stand at full length and fill the space from bottom to top. The adaptation of design and color to prescribed space was (and is) the primary requisite of good decoration; and the early artist was accounted a success or a failure just in proportion as he accepted or rejected this requisite.

Centuries after the period of Primitive Man—no one knows how many centuries—when civilization had become established on the banks of the Nile, we find pottery, household utensils, weapons of warfare, furniture, embroideries, walls of temples and walls of tombs, all covered with patterns, figures, and colors. The carvings and paintings are better in execution, but not unlike those of more barbaric times. And the artist here in Egypt, like his predecessor in the Stone Age, is concerned with filling spaces decoratively. To be sure the king in his chariot surrounded by his bowmen, the flying enemy, the files of prisoners bearing tribute, the convocation of the gods, the scenes from royal and humble life, are all records of history, religion, or custom. The painter is saying something, illustrating something, with his figures and groups and colors; but how careful he is that he shall say it gracefully, pleasing the eye as well as the mind. The composition usually runs in long tiers or bands and the spaces are filled with standing or moving figures. The open spots about

XXIII.—BONIFAZIO VERONESE, Moses Saved from the Nile. Brera, Milan.

the figures are dotted with accessory objects, such as palms, fruits, implements, cartouches—all decorative in form or color. Everywhere in the Egyptian temple the hieroglyphs appeared in bands and rows—a text explanatory of the subject, but introduced in such a manner that no space in the picture should look empty or wanting in balance.

Assyrian art tells us the same tale. The alabaster slabs that lined the palace walls of Nineveh were all cut of one size, and the colored bas-reliefs upon them picturing warriors, chariots, horses, dogs, hunting scenes, battle scenes, and sacred scenes conformed to that size. Trees and city ramparts and rivers were used as accessory objects, and often the cuneiform inscriptions ran across them and held them together like a veil of atmosphere. With Greek art this decorative filling-of-space reached its highest point in the ancient world. You cannot to-day take up a red-figured vase, a silver coin, or an engraved gem without being conscious that the artist's first thought was how to fill the given space effectively. There is little attempt at fitting a round stone into a square hole. The whole surface of the vase, the coin, or the gem is covered with a regard for the general form of the space decorated. A Greek coin almost always shows good decorative effect, because the disk is completely filled with a round profile; an American coin usually shows poor decorati effect because the space is not filled with one large object, but is huddled full of small dates, figures, stars, liberty - caps, and shields. The Greek die-sinker is influenced solely by decorative appearance, whereas the American die-sinker or his employer wants to tell you on a ten-cent piece all about the constitution, the flag, and the magnificent freedom and general excellence of the greatest republic on earth.

Not alone with small objects was the Greek a decorative workman. The wall-paintings, the sculpture, the architecture, all exemplified his skill in space-filling. It was no mere accident that the figures in the highest part of a Parthenon pediment were shown standing, and that they were seated or reclining in the lower angles. There was a pedimental form to fill with figures, and Pheidias would not have been Pheidias had he not placed the figures so that they would fill the space gracefully, easily, and with no loss of dignity in their attitudes. Just so with the Parthenon frieze of Athenian youths on horseback. How gracefully they ride ! And how well adapted the moving train of horsemen to the long, lane-like frieze that conducts them around the temple. It is obvious enough that the sculptor had to consider the field upon which he worked, and he had to fill it so that it would first of all be beautiful to the eye.

The step from ancient to modern art is a long one, but the decorating motive did not die with the Greeks. The Gothic age had perhaps more need for it than the age of Pericles. When painting began to rise in Italy, the chief patron of it was the all-powerful Church. At that time artists were not artists, in name at least. They were mechanics, members of trades-unions called guilds, and were hired to do certain kinds of work like carpenters, masons, stone-cutters, and other mechanics. The painter at that time was often a layer of colors, a gilder of altar-pieces, a modeller in clay, a hewer of marble, a goldsmith, a frame-maker—all in one. When the church was built he was called in to decorate it—that is, to make it beautiful to look at, attractive in appearance. There were certain architectural spaces—ovals, triangles, squares, panels—certain recesses in the apse, the dome, the ceiling, that had to be filled with carvings, designs, pictures. He filled them, and he was praised or criticised as he filled those spaces decoratively or otherwise. He was a decorator pure and simple. Then came Giotto. The same kind of spaces needed filling, but Giotto filled them better than his predecessors. His decorative sense was larger, his taste in color more refined ; and he could draw a figure nobler and with more flexibility as regards its muscular play and action. Painting advanced with a bound. It did not do so because of Giotto's subjects, because he painted the traditional Church themes like those before him ; but because Giotto was, for his time, a great craftsman.

A hundred or more years later came Masaccio. Art was once more pushed suddenly forward, for Masaccio rounded the archaic line, drew drapery with ease, fathomed the tones of colors, gave light-and-shade, perspective, values. Then another hundred years to Michael Angelo and Raphael. With these two last-named artists drawing reached a great height. It could not at that time be carried further, and no painters in Florence were so famed for drawing and composition as Michael Angelo and Raphael. They filled space quite perfectly with lines and forms. (Plates 21 and 28.)

Contemporary with Michael Angelo and Raphael lived Leonardo da Vinci. He was an excellent draughtsman but you do not often hear him spoken of as such. His fame rests largely upon his discovery and mastery of light-and-shade. Here was something new with which to fill space. It made no difference that at this time painting often came down from the apse and the ceiling and spread itself upon canvas and wooden panel to make what we to-day call the easel picture. The decorative motive was not lost sight of for a moment. Leonardo was just as solicitous that the panel should be decoratively beautiful as the wall fresco, and he made it beautiful by his mystery of light-and-shade, by his figures and colors. He was for Florence the perfect craftsman, and many students followed his initiative. Then came Correggio at Parma (Plate 8) and Giorgione at Venice (Plate 24), varying the use of light-and-shade and making of it a magnificent background upon which to weave colors. These three men for Italy perfected and completed the decorative use of light-and-shade, and you will always hear them spoken of as the masters of chiaroscuro, the inventors of composition by masses of light and dark.

One moment more to the school of Venice! You will remember that from her infancy Venice was a trader with the East. She was the carrier by sea, the broker, between Europe and that realm of Mahomet lying back of Constantinople which has never known any other art than colored ornament. This Moslem empire and its color-glamour had its influence upon the Venetians through their ships and traders, and when the painters began the fabrication of altar-pieces and mosaics for the Venetian churches it was not line or form or light or shade that primarily interested them. It was color—the color of the old decadent Eastern world—to which they were devoted. The Bellinis began it, their pupils Giorgione and Titian made it glorious, Paolo Veronese gave it final brilliancy and splendor. (Plates 5 and 14.) Again the height was reached.   Space-filling at Venice was done primarily by masses of color, and to-day you will always hear the Venetians spoken of as the great colorists in art.

Now have you noticed that I have given you, in this little outline of art-history, the names of the great masters in painting ?   Have you noticed that the rise of that greatest school of all, the Italian, can be adequately explained on purely decorative grounds ? Art was great in Italy primarily because the Italians were great technicians, great decorators, great space-fillers.   If you will turn back and read their lives, their adventures, and their quarrels among themselves you will discover that they were not wholly absorbed by the Madonnas and Holy Families and the religious sentiment of art.   Many of them had piety and strong belief, and some of them had neither the one nor the other.   The subjects were dealt out to all of them alike by the Church ; but the manner in which they should be painted was something taught in the *bottega* of the master, something dictated in each case by the space (the wall or altar) which had to be decorated.

Even the pietists like Fra Angelico were not free of obligation to the decorative.   Nor did a single one of them ever wish to be free.   Whether they believed in religion or not, whether they had pietistic sentiment or not, they all believed in the beauty of good

form and good color. If you will look again at
Andrea del Sarto's Holy Families you will see little
holiness about them or in them. They are only
Florentine people posed in traditional attitudes,
with Andrea's wife enacting the part of the Madonna. But they are not wanting in decorative
charm. Andrea knew how to fill space if not how
to paint soul, and it was because he did fill space
beautifully in the convent of the Annunziata that his
townspeople called him "the faultless painter." No
one ever referred to him as "the faultless thinker"
or "the faultless sentimentalist" or "the pietistic
painter."

If you will look again at the pictures of Titian you
will see only handsome, well-fed, richly robed Venetians. Their brows are not burdened with Christian
ecstasy nor their faces furrowed with classic thought.
There is little to them but fine form and fine color.
And yet I venture to think that Titian, taking him
for all in all, was the greatest painter known to history. It was by and with such men—men devoted to
the material and technical side of their art—that
Italian craftsmanship rose step by step through three
hundred years of severe training until the Renaissance height was reached and great art was the result.
The pictorial voice of Italy would never have been
heard in this world had it not been for the decorative
skill of the workman, the craftsman of the Renais-

sance, the man we to-day call a technician. And
from beginning to end the first consideration of Italian art was not religion, nor nature, nor the ideal nor
the classic, but rather the making of a beautiful decoration by the use of lines, lights, shadows, and
colors.

I am aware that you regard all this as decidedly
heterodox, and possibly you may think I am distorting the facts to make a point in argument. But
no. I am stating the artist's contention, giving his
idea of the development of art—the view held by
the ancients and still upheld to-day by the moderns. But let me ramble on a little further, and consider this matter negatively. You know that with
Raphael, Michael Angelo, and Titian art in Italy
reached its climax, and that after them came that
deluge known to history as the Decadence. But
why was there a decadence? What caused it?
Nothing more nor less than that the followers of the
great men came to regard craftsmanship as something of a trick to be readily picked up, and failed
to study with the severity of the early men. They
thought to be technicians without labor, to gain fa-
cility without skill, to produce great pictures without knowledge. Their predecessors had achieved
technique, and the followers thought they had nothing
to do but help themselves to the result without both.
ering about going to the fountain-head. So they

XXIV.—GIORGIONE, Madonna and Saints. Cathedral, Castelfranco.

tried to combine certain line-effects of Raphael with Titian's color and Correggio's light-and-shade. Of course this attempt at a unity of technical excellences was an absurdity. Then, too, they began to think that the sublime or sentimental subject was worth more than good workmanship, and that Michael Angelo's greatness lay in his mystery-haunted figures, as Raphael's in his round-faced Madonnas. So they began copying these features, too. And as a result there appeared the ponderous scowling Titans of Salviati and Vasari, the sugary, empty-headed Madonnas of Carlo Dolci and Sassoferrato. They could not draw or paint like the great masters, because their hands had not been thoroughly trained; they could not design decoratively, because their taste had become corrupted; they could not think effectively, because they were following other people's ideas rather than their own. No wonder there was decadence. It would have been very strange had there been anything else.

Two hundred years of this meretricious art followed the downfall of the Renaissance. During those centuries painting in Europe lay barren, save in some exceptional spots. It flourished in Holland with Rembrandt; it flourished in Flanders with Rubens; it flourished in Spain with Velasquez. Why did it flourish? If I were searching the entire history of painting I could not name for you three greater technicians than Rembrandt, Rubens, and Velasquez. With Titian, they are the great masters of the craft. Art always flourishes in the hands of the skilled craftsman; it always languishes in the hands of the unskilled craftsman. And it is necessary to insist upon it again that all these men were workmen, working with the decorative sense uppermost. They were artists, too—artists who expressed great thoughts, sentiments, and emotions, particularly Rembrandt; but they never would have been artists, they never would have represented any fact or thought worth considering, had they not been, first of all, decorative workmen.

But you may say we have changed all that. The painter in those days was only a court dependant—a varlet of the king—not different from cabinet-makers, stone-cutters, and other mechanics; but to-day he is an independent citizen, a creative genius, a teacher of mankind, an influencer and moulder of public opinion. Yes; but the picture is still the picture. And custom may change the painter's skin, but not his nature. He is still a skilled workman at heart, or at least would be such. And his main aim is decorative craftsmanship. Modern painting gives it proof. It is said, and truly enough, that art has advanced in this century. Why has it advanced? Simply because it has taken hold of the old technical and decorative problems, and tried to better them.

In France, Ingres was doing his best to draw like Raphael, when Delacroix came to the front with a new kind of drawing. Instead of line he substituted the patch of color, and made the outer rim elastic, movable, life-like. Corot, Rousseau, and the land-scape painters ; Courbet, Millet, and Manet, the *genre* painters, helped complete it. Art under them rose rapidly, and the truth of nature was more nearly approximated.

But the light was too dull, the shadows too black. A new man came to the front to revise and re-edit the light and shade of Leonardo, Correggio, and Rembrandt. That man was Monet, the so-called impressionist. He changed the whole pitch of light by transposing the scale, and giving both lights and darks a higher register. And has not the rich deep color of the old Venetians been revised too ? Look about you at the high keys of color that greet you in every modern picture exhibition. Claude Monet, whom people smiled at a dozen years ago, but are now calling a genius, is responsible for this high scale of color and light. He has transformed the whole decorative aspect of landscape painting, by study-ing the intermixture and play of pigments. We are now seeing colors in art that approximate, at least, the colors of nature ; and they are just as beautiful decoratively as the old ones, only we are not yet ac-customed to them.

Painting advances, breaks out new sails, and enters upon new seas with such new knowledge of materials. And of course some of the energy put into the study is to enable the painters to show a truer life and nature than ever before ; but we are not to forget that there is beauty also in the new pitch of light and color and that the painter is using them with a decorative purpose. Indeed it would be easy to demonstrate that no present-day painter begins upon an oval, a square, a triangle of wood or canvas, without first planning how to fill that space gracefully with forms, lights, and colors. These nineteenth-century painters have had few wall-spaces to fill, but it has already been suggested that the decorative tradition has descended to them, and that they are as considerate about filling a panel or canvas as ever the old men were considerate about filling an apse or spandrel.

But I fancy you are ready to stop me by protesting that these motives are too material, too mechanical. You will perhaps insist that true art is above all this petty planning, squaring, measuring, space-filling ; that genius knows not method, and that the ideal out-soars the base materials that would hold it down to earth. There are those who believe that inspiration dictates with the voice of an angel and that the hand of the poet or painter but obeys the voice ; there are those who believe there is no labor or plan or de-

XXV.—REYNOLDS, Lady Cockburn and Family. National Gallery, London.

sign or foundation in the work of art. And it is true
that oftentimes painting and poetry appear so effort-
less that we think them spontaneous and unpremedi-
tated. But those are always the works that have been
slaved over the most. Every great work of art is
based in technical knowledge and has the skilled
workman back of it. And many are the poets born
by nature, yet lacking the accomplishment of verse.
Did you ever read a great piece of prose or poetry written by a man ignorant of grammar and the rhythmical
construction of sentences ? Did you ever hear of a
good piece of architecture built by a man who knew
not plans, scales, and proportions ? Did you ever see
a great picture painted by a man who could not draw
decently or lay color harmoniously ? We are quite
right in admiring the feeling, the enthusiasm, yes,
the inspiration, if you prefer that word, of some
great violinist over his instrument ; but we should
not forget the training of the hand, the many years
of dealing with the material that made enthusiasm
and feeling possible. How much of them should
we have heard had the hand remained untrained ?
Shelley's poetic thoughts, yes, but Shelley's sense of
melody, his knowledge of rhythm, his general mastery of words and sentences, gave them meaning to
the world. And so, too, while we admire Tintoretto's fertility of resource and his bounding imagination we should not overlook the fact that it was his

absolute skill of hand, his knowledge of line **and** light and color, that made an idyl of the "Ariadne and Bacchus" and an epic of that great maëlstrom composition the "Paradise."

Materials, craftsmanship, the decorative sense which requires that a man's work shall be interesting in itself, are the very bases of art; and we often go astray in our judgments by not considering them. We have with us to-day one of the best literary technicians of the nineteenth century—Mr. James the novelist. It can hardly be contended that he is a very popular novelist. We sometimes read outbreaks in newspaper or magazine columns to the effect that he is not much of a story-teller, has not much of a plot. That is the complaint of the average person in the picture-gallery when he stands face to face with a Whistler nocturne. He wants what the artist does not care to paint. Mr. Whistler and Mr. James are both very well acquainted with the pretty face and the romantic story, but they choose to ignore them. The average person may read a novel by Mr. James and keep asking : What does it mean ? but if Mr. James were at his elbow and disposed to ask questions he would certainly inquire : How does it read ?

It may be admitted, if you please, that the insistence upon the decorative use of language with Mr. James or with Mr. Swinburne is excessive. And so, too, the followers of Mr. Whistler, if not the leader himself, may be thought to refine color and mystify tone and shadow into a meaningless fog of pigments. Any principle, however good in itself, may be rendered ridiculous by extravagance in its application. But the followers of the decorative are not the only ones who go beyond the normal. Painters who are given to "ideas in art" oftentimes fly to the other extreme and neglect the decorative altogether. Mr. Holman Hunt, for example, will hardly be accused of not having enough ideas and meaning in his Palestine pictures, and just as certainly he will not be accused of pandering to the decorative. His drawing, coloring, painting, surfaces, are anything but pleasing. Nor does anyone doubt that Walt Whitman has put forth some poetic ideas as great as any in American literature, but the form in which he has sent them forth is far enough removed from the rhythmical. You read him and question perhaps whether he is a great poet or a solemn impostor just because he trusts his thoughts to bad drawing, crude coloring, and incoherent composition, just because he dispenses with the decorative.

Now you will please not understand me as saying that it makes no difference what you say if you but say it well, or that the setting is nobler or better than the gem itself. It is not necessary to rush to either extreme of statement. Some artists there be who make sweeping claims for the decorative, and so far as they themselves are concerned they are doubtless in the right. That is to say, form and color, in graceful combinations, make one kind of painting ; but we need not straightway conclude that it is the only kind of painting. It has been suggested already that music and poetry may have something more to them than melodious sounds that fall sweetly on the ear ; and that painting may have another mission than that of pleasing the eye with sensuous lines and colors. The ultimate end of painting is perhaps the expression of emotional feeling ; and I am not now contending for superlative and final art in the Persian-rug picture made up of subtle lights and tones of colors. But it may be reasonably insisted that it is better for the picture— no matter what its ulterior meaning—that it should first of all be pleasing to the eye and decoratively attractive. Certainly that is the way all the great artists of the world have thought and wrought, from the man of the Stone Age who first decorated pottery to the American of to-day who is concerned with filling space upon panel or canvas.

And this decorative motive, which was the first consideration, remains to the last the most enduring feature of art. The history of a marble or a picture may be lost ; its subject or theme may be forgotten ; what it meant or signified to a past generation may be incomprehensible to a present generation ; but what it *looks* is substantially the same for all times

XXVI.—CLAUDE LORRAINE, Flight into Egypt.

and all peoples. What, I wonder, makes the glory
of the " Venus of Milo "—the fact that she is a Venus? It has been gravely questioned, is still questioned, just what character that figure is intended to
personify ; but it has never been doubted that it is a
wonderful piece of line and form—something beautiful to look upon. What makes the glory of Titian's
" Sacred and Profane Love "? There is nothing
either sacred or profane about it; the title is a mis-
nomer—something attached to the picture long after
the painter's death—and no one knows what Titian
intended to say in the picture. But is the picture
less beautiful for that? It is a splendid panel of
form and color; any name or no name could not
render it less splendid. Its decorative quality is
quite perfect. All those altar-pieces, frescoes, and
mosaics in the Italian churches—how much meaning
have they and their sacred subjects for the unbeliev-
ing art-lover of to-day! Very little indeed ; but
how beautiful they are to look upon just as pictures! (Plates 23 and 27). Who really cares to-day
for the characters of Lear, Hamlet, and Macbeth
as compared with the deathless language of their
decorative setting! Who does not care for Shakespeare's jewelled sentences!

It is the common experience of art-lovers that the
more they study pictures the more certainly do they
lose interest in the theme or narrative illustrated.
The historical or poetical incident portrayed fades

into insignificance beside well-drawn forms and impressive schemes of color. No one who knows much about painting ever looks twice for the meaning of a Watteau or a Lancret group. The only meaning of it lies in its vivacity and gayety expressed in color and handling. Even where the meaning is important, as in Reynolds's "Lady Cockburn and Family" (Plate 25) or Leighton's "Summer Moon," it is not possible to overlook or ignore the intertwining and blending of the group in both form and color, which makes it so attractive decoratively.

Such in brief is the artist's view of art. It is firmly based upon the decorative, though all artists do not advocate it to the extinction of every other feature of the painting. On the contrary there are many who believe in sentiment, feeling, and emotional expression as the final aim. And some there are who stickle for the value of history, archæology, and story, as others for the value of the natural and the real. Indeed, there are several kinds of painting, representing several different points of view, and if we would cultivate catholicity of taste we should consider them all. There is a large body of intelligent people in this world who are even heretical enough to believe that art has some value as illustration; and since we have given the painter's contention, perhaps it would be as well that we now state the case for the other side.

CHAPTER VI

SUBJECT IN PAINTING

It has been intimated, more than once in these lectures, that the artist, deep down in his heart, has no great respect for the public's taste concerning works of art. He has always arrogated to himself and his fellows the exclusive right of saying what was and what was not art ; and he would have us believe that after all art is made only for the appreciation of artists. Such a feeling is comforting and comfortable, no doubt. It possibly pervades branches of industry other than the arts. The shoemaker probably feels that he knows more about shoes than the people that wear them and the cook more about dinners than the people that eat them ; but neither of them would contend that shoes were made only for shoemakers or dinners only for cooks. Nor can the contention of art exclusively for the artist be made good save in the extravagant atmosphere of the art-school. Unless the picture appeals to someone without the studio, unless it is accepted by someone in the outside world, its excuse for being would seem to be very slight. The work may please the worker and he may be as absorbed and happy in his occupation as a child making sand houses on the sea-shore ; but in neither case is energy put to a profitable purpose. An author writes a book to be read by the public, and an orator speaks to be heard by the public ; why should not a painter paint to be seen by the public ?

And the audience that sees has something to say about what the painter shall paint. It creates in large measure the demand which the artist supplies. I am aware that oftentimes the contrary is maintained and it is asserted that the artist sets the pace and directs the public taste. Sometimes he does, but he is influenced more or less by his audience. The demand for work has always come from those who could pay for it, and the patron usually insists upon having his views incorporated in the work. The history of painter and patron in the past rather confirms this. No doubt Michael Angelo had some contempt for the art views of Julius II., but he painted the Sistine ceiling as the Pope requested. And probably Rubens thought his Jesuit patrons in Flanders an ignorant pack of priests, but he painted the themes and subjects they designated. The subject—aye—there's the rub ! For the public will have it and the painters will hate it—that is to say, some of the modern painters have come to hate it apparently for no other reason than that the public likes it. Of recent years there has arisen a cry of " art for art's sake "—that is to say, art in the form, color, and workmanship, but

XXVII.—TINTORETTO, Marriage in Cana. S. M. della Salute, Venice.

not in the thought or subject—and many artists have given their unqualified support to the dogma. In upholding the charm of the decorative they are prone to deny charm to anything and everything else. Form and color, they alone make a picture, and all else is philistine sentiment—the very leather and prunello of art.

It is not to be denied that this contention of the painter is right enough so far as it affirms the importance of the decorative. Form and color do make art, and that too with slight reference to subject-meaning; but we may question the assumption that there is no other form of art, and that the subject and what art may mean to us are matters of no importance. We have already considered the different kinds of painting that are produced by painters who think and paint in different ways. "Art is in the look," says Whistler; "No, it is in the thought," says Millet; Vibert in his pictures seems to believe it is the subject that counts; and if Meissonier were alive he would certainly insist upon it that art consists in realizing the model—in painting a boot you could pull off or a spur you could put on. But it must be apparent to you that each one of these men, while exploiting his own preference, is possibly exploiting his own limitation. No doubt each one of them believes there is nothing to be seen beyond where he has travelled.

But there is something too much of "my way is the only way" in these views of painting. Not perhaps too much for the men themselves, because a person usually succeeds better who believes implicitly in himself and is convinced by his own convictions; but too much perhaps for those who have nothing to do with production, who have to do only with the enjoyment of things produced. Individually we may be willing to admit that neither the subject nor the realistic portrayal of nature interests us so much as the look of a picture and what it may express in thought or sentiment; but it would be idle for us to ignore the fact that four-fifths of the people who are looking at pictures are interested only in subject and that perhaps two-thirds of the painters who are painting them are intent only upon doing something realistic. It is possible to influence and persuade these many dwellers in Philistia, if you choose so to regard them, but they cannot be pushed aside contemptuously.

And sometimes the persuasion of the artist is in direct defiance of the rational. The "no-subject" cry of some present-day writers of fiction will perhaps illustrate this. What shall we say, for instance, to the extravagance of those who tell us that in writing nothing which teaches, argues, or expounds is "literature"; that "literature" consists in the writing of something clever about nothing, and that when the thing said becomes of importance the work ceases to be literary. The inference is, of course, that history and essay step down and out in favor of poetry and fiction ; that Richard Le Gallienne's sensuous cadences and Henry Harland's delightful ping-pong conversations are "literature"; but not Macaulay's history and De Quincey's essays. Are we to believe that there is no art in Bossuet's oration over the great Condé because it preaches ; no art in Taine's philosophy because it teaches ? It is true enough that there is art in the skilful use of the adjective, in the glow of words, and in the slip of sentences ; but why is there not art also in the handling of an idea, in the development of a subject, in a point of view ? Why is it necessary to let the sense out of everything before it becomes artistic ? Practically it is not possible to separate the mental from the mechanical. The mind guides the hand, and both are but manifestations of an individuality. How shall you distinguish Shakespeare the thinker from Shakespeare the dramatic writer ? How shall you separate emotional thinking from its sequence, enthusiastic craftsmanship ? People are not convinced by the argument for art in the method but not in the mind or the material.

Mr. Whistler, speaking for painting, is scarcely less extravagant than the writers. "As music is the poetry of sound, so is painting the poetry of sight, and the subject-matter has nothing to do with the harmony of sound or of color. Art should stand alone and appeal to the artistic sense of eye or ear without confounding this with emotions entirely foreign to it, as devotion, pity, love, patriotism, and the like." Thus Mr. Whistler; and again there is a measure of pungent pertinence in the remark. Painting should appeal primarily to " the artistic sense of eye," but not necessarily to that alone. There is no reason why it should not have a meaning and express a feeling or a sentiment about something besides form and color. Even music appeals to something more than the ear. It suggests a feeling, an association. If it be true that it has no idea or sentiment, why do we grow sad over Siegfried's Death March, or elated over that last upward burst of song in the dungeon scene from " Faust"? Why do we become emotional or sentimental or romantic over a symphony by Beethoven? If we wish meaningless sound we must take the æolian harp or the hum of the wind through pine needles or the roar of the sea breaking on the beach; and perhaps each of these seems beautiful to us largely because it suggests something like a human moan or wail.

Just so there may be a suggestion or meaning behind the most decorative of pictures. Every picture, if it be coherent at all, illustrates, represents, or expresses some fact, thought, or feeling. However shadowy the trees of the no-subject artist, however vague and ghost-like the figures of a symphonist in paint, we see and recognize the trees and the figures. The lines, lights, and colors are so placed that they illustrate subjects, namely, trees and figures ; they convey to us a meaning, and if they are so indefinite that we cannot distinguish trees from figures, rocks from grass, or water from sky, then the picture is not a picture, but merely a dash of variegated colors. Two dead fish upon a plank and behind them an iron pot —the picture that Vollon has painted for us—has, as a picture, perhaps as little subject about it as the most confirmed modern could desire ; yet it is no less a subject. We recognize the pot, the plank, the fish readily enough. Smear the canvas so that we have only streaks of gray and black, and the subject is gone and with it the picture. It is then only a medley of pigment which may be rather interesting as a color-spot, but is no more of a picture than so much color rubbed on the panel of a door.

Mr. Whistler may call one of his small canvases of the open sea a symphony in blue or gray or catalogue it by any other fantastic name he chooses ; but the fact remains that his few touches of the brush give us not only the form and color of the sea, but suggest to us the great ocean tossing after storm —rolling moodily under gray skies. The painter intended that such a meaning should be suggested. If he had not defined his sea and sky so that we could recognize them his canvas might still be a pretty piece of blue and gray, and it might be a "symphony"; but it would not be a picture. It would not picture anything; it would be merely pigment again.

And even an art-for-art's-sake devotee might wonder why Mr. Whistler should fight wind-mills about "devotion, pity, love and patriotism" in pictures. Are the altar-pieces of the early Italians the worse for being filled with what people choose to think true "devotion"? Would the pictures by Filippino or Botticelli be the better if the pietistic sentiment were eliminated and a smiling Froufrou took the place of the sad-faced Madonna? Consider for a moment that splendid family group kneeling in the altar-piece of the Pesaro family by Titian, and then ask yourself if the suggestion of devotion here is any more objectionable than the spirit of frivolity or gayety in a scene from the ballet by Degas. Some years ago there was a rather interesting picture by Dagnan-Bouveret in the Salon, called "The Conscripts"—a picture showing a squad of youths marching down the street to the sound of drum-beats, with the tricolor flying over their heads. The sentiment of it was undoubtedly patriotic, and crowds stood about it day by day as long as the exhibition remained open. Would Mr. Whistler condemn it for either its patriotism or its popularity? If so, why not the "Surrender at Breda" by Velasquez? That, too, smacks of military glory, and I doubt not had its crowds of Spaniards staring at it in the past as Dagnan-Bouveret's picture in the present. And why not put Rembrandt's "Night Watch," and Frans Hals's Shooting Companies at Haarlem in the same pillory? They are full of uniforms, flags, drums and guns, and they are stuffed with patriotism, civic pride and burgher conceit; but, oddly enough, we find no painter-writer abusing them on that account. Why? Because they are not lacking in decorative quality; they are superb as form and color.

So it seems then that Velasquez, Frans Hals, and Rembrandt shall go scot-free for perpetrating what is adjudged little short of a crime in Sir John Millais and George Boughton. Which is it, then, the presence of the devotional and the patriotic or the absence of the decorative that really excites the wrath of the Whistlerians? Possibly what their spokesmen meant to say was that in modern painting there is too much insistence upon the theme, the subject, the story told; that artistic qualities of form and color are ignored, pushed aside, overlooked in favor of the incident set forth; that painting is not a mere vehicle for illustrating poetry, fiction, religion, or history; that it has qualities peculiarly its own, which are entitled to quite as much consideration as the thought or theme which may be illustrated. And all of that would be true enough. The decorative phase of art is quite as important as the illustrative, but why are not both important? Why and how do they conflict with one another?

But, to return to our original contention, expressive painting cannot get on without a thought and a theme. It must represent or illustrate something. And if we should cast out all the pictures that have an expressive meaning we should do away with almost all the art of the past. Certainly all descriptive art would have to go. Historical canvases, we are told, are only "illustrative" anyway, and not art pure and simple. But just where shall the line be drawn between what is historical and what is not historical? A canvas of Napoleon retreating from Russia is illustrative—historical beyond doubt; but how does Meissonier's portrait of Napoleon riding at the head of his bedraggled columns differ from Mr. Whistler's picture of a blacksmith at his forge? One is the likeness of a famous general in time of war, the other is the likeness of a common blacksmith in time of peace; but both canvases are biographical, and therefore historical. A picture of the field of Gravelotte or the palace at Versailles might serve as an illustration of the political history of France; but a wheat stack and a row of poplars by Monet, a

XXVIII.—RAPHAEL, Sistine Madonna. Dresden Gallery.

wood-chopper or a gleaner by Millet, why do they not equally well illustrate the social and agricultural history of France? There is really no point where one can stop. Everything that can be recognized at all in a painting is more or less illustrative of history, fact or incident. And there is no reason why modernity should strain at an interesting subject because it happens to be political history, and swallow a stupid one because it happens to be social history. Titian, Rubens, and Velasquez did not do it. Each one of them painted the life and history of his time, not in portraiture alone, but in battle scene and court ceremony. And famous canvases they made of them, too. Can it be thought for a moment that the subjects were detrimental to the artists or their art? Evidently the painters themselves did not think so.

And is the church art of Italy to go, too, because it illustrates the biblical narratives? Without doubt it is the most complete expression of painting we have ever known, the most perfect in decorative charm, the most satisfactory in expressive meaning. What if it did teach the Bible to those who could not read! Did it not also adorn the interior of churches, and fulfil the modern requirements of painting by its beauty of form and color? And if it be true that art consists not in devotion or patriotism, but in drawing the nude figure, what difference does it make whether you draw that of Adam lying upon the edge of the world as Michael Angelo, or that of a dead unknown lying upon a hospital slab as Rembrandt? If the female figure be insisted upon as the acme of graceful line and delicate color, why cannot these be shown in a " Susanna at the Bath " as well as in a " Venus " or an " Olympe " ? Some years ago Mr. Whistler painted the figure of a girl in white standing at full length upon a white bear-skin, and the result was called " The White Girl." It is a study in whites, and his followers might count it a symphony in white without making much more of it than a clever exposition of painter's values. In Venice, some centuries ago, Palma Vecchio painted the figure of a girl in rich browns standing at full length upon guns, and called the result "Santa Barbara." (Frontispiece.) As a symphony, as a study in color-harmony, as a piece of drawing and painting, it is irreproachable. It is decoratively all that could be desired. Yes ; and there is something more to it. The figure expresses superb dignity, nobility, and repose ; it is the perfect type of woman ; and in addition the picture has illustrated to the mob for many years the story of Santa Barbara the martyr. Both pictures are true enough art, delightful each in its way ; but which is the more complete ? And would you have the meaning knocked out of Palma's picture, would you have it reduced to a mere symphony of brown and gold—something you might catalogue as "The Brown Girl"? Suppose, for argument's sake, we admit that calling it Santa Barbara does not help it in any way; but does it injure it in any way? Certainly not.

Nor is it worth while to accept an allegorical figure by Fantin-Latour or a nursing mother by Degas and then quarrel with the meaning of a "Madonna" by Bellini (Plate 7) or a "St. Catherine" by Sodoma. The use of the latter pictures by the Church to point a moral or adorn a tale does not invalidate their art, nor does the name attached to them blind anyone to their harmony of form, light, and color. We may be certain that those Renaissance men were just as much interested in the decorative side of their art as the moderns. They were expert technicians with a fine sense of line and color. Every feature of the Madonna's face, form or costume, the fall of a robe, the sparkle of a gem, the play of light upon hair or nude shoulder, the depth and resonance of colors, were seized upon for decorative effect; but the emotions of "devotion, pity and the like," which Mr. Whistler insists are quite foreign to art, did not disturb them in any way. They used them as they pleased and still made beautiful pictures.

Just so with the Dutchmen at the north. They painted portraits, interiors, *fête* scenes, marines—all things that related to Holland—and they were very

intent upon giving the realistic appearance of everything so that anyone could divine the meaning ; but
they did not neglect the decorative nor quarrel about
the subjects of their canvases.   The fine conversation-
pictures of Terburg or the interiors of Steen or the
portraits of Hals (Plate 22) need no apology for their
purely artistic qualities.   Every face or hand or figure, every scrap of light or color, has the most made
of it.   The painters wrung all the hues possible out
of silks and satins, caught all the sparkle of glass,
all the sheen of pots and dishes ; but they did not
think to win entirely by virtue of these qualities.
They cared something for their subject and insisted
upon its truth of representation and illustration, too.

And what of the landscape ? Are we to cast out
the historical productions of Claude and Turner
(Plates 11 and 26) because they are supposed to represent ancient Italy or classic Greece ? What if
Turner does paint a picture of Venice in which people may recognize some things Venetian, does that
mar his painting of light, air, sky, and color, or dim
the decorative splendor of the landscape in any way ?
Those splendid Venetian sunsets with scarlet clouds
waving and flaming far up the zenith, their crimson
reflection in the waters of the lagoons, the golden atmosphere that never painter yet painted, how are
they harmed by the stray sunshafts that flush pink
the familiar top of the San Marco campanile or gild

XXIX.—BOTTICELLI, Allegory of Spring. Academy, Florence.

into recognition the great silver domes of the Salute ? And if a modern paint a patch of mid-ocean without a name how much greater as art are his sea-waves than the waves of Claude shown in a seaport of France ? What harm does the " seaport " and " France " do the picture ? We have recently had some very beautiful studies of color, light, and air by Claude Monet which he has called " Rouen Cathedral " and " Westminster Bridge." They are much vaguer in outline than Turner or Claude would have painted them ; but they picture historical structures and might be called historical landscapes with as much reason as Turner's " Bay of Baiæ " or Claude's " Queen of Sheba."

But the chief quarrel of the modern is with the story-telling subject—the sentimental or funny incident in paint—of which we see enough and to spare at every new exhibition. This too is historical art in a way. For the *genre* subjects of the present time are history in the little—personal incidents usually, but nevertheless the history of the people. And yet it must be acknowledged that there is some reason for waging war against this kind of art as we find it to-day. Not that the story in itself is necessarily objectionable. If we are not interested in its incident perhaps we can enjoy its decorative qualities. The " Sacred and Profane Love " by Titian, which I have already mentioned, certainly had a literary meaning

at one time, but to-day the allegory is lost to us and
the picture lives by virtue of its fine form and color—
the allegory in no way injuring its decorative qualities.
Nor are the stories of Jan Steen or Van der Meer
of Delft or Teniers objectionable in their pictures.
You will hear no modern railing against them, for
the very good reason that the pictures are excellent
pieces of workmanship and exceptionally beautiful in
surfaces, handling, color, light and atmosphere. But
the present-day story-teller with a paint-brush is not
so good a workman as the Dutchmen. He slurs the
decorative and throws all the interest of his picture
upon the incident portrayed, and lets form and color
go lame, blind and halt if they choose. There is little
to be said in praise of his work. The tawdry colors
and the card-board figures with which his stories are
told condemn them at the start. Yet the public,
seeing not the cheapness of the method, applauds the
incident portrayed and thus endorses a lame and halt-
ing art. It is this that stirs the wrath of the art-for-
art's-sake advocates and leads to their extravagance
of statement.

It is the Marcus Stones, the Viberts, and the De-
freggers of painting who have brought the story into
contempt and caused the opposition to it. That the
"unco guid" Sunday-school incident or the horse-
play of the grinning Tyrolean peasant, or the red-
robed monk story should pass current as art while the

peasants of Millet, the landscapes of Corot, the marines of Whistler should be sneered at as impressionistic or "faddish," was more than the artistic brotherhood could bear. It took up the cudgels for more art and less literature, and in knocking the silly incident in the head, it also tried to knock in the head every other incident in the art-world. This was perhaps an error. For the subject is not necessarily silly except in the hands of the whipper-snapper painter. There is nothing silly about the "Moses saved from the Nile" (Plate 23) by Bonifazio, or the "Miracle of the Slave" (Plate 15) by Tintoretto, or the "Good Samaritan" by Rembrandt, or the "Garden of Love" by Rubens, or the "Shepherds in Arcadia" (Plate 30) by Poussin. Oh, yes; the old masters could paint stories when it pleased them to do so. They were religious and classic stories—themes hallowed by tradition—but not differing in other respects from the stories of to-day. They painted them well and with great decorative skill and therefore you never hear any painter decrying them; but, so far as their legitimacy or illegitimacy is concerned, they were not different from the "Love and Death" of Mr. Watts or the "Beguiling of Merlin" by Sir Edward Burne-Jones or the "Blind Fiddler" by Sir David Wilkie.

But we must not push our argument too hard, for we are not the special advocates of the story-picture.

Nor should we, while stating the contention of the public for the subject-picture, be unjust to the contention of the painter for the decorative picture. It is true enough that the religious or classic theme of Renaissance art is not its most enduring quality with us to-day. The pictures live more by their excellences of form and color than by their subjects. Still the painters found no great hardship in having to paint designated themes. They worked easily under imposed conditions. When Mantegna was asked to paint a chapel in the Eremitani at Padua and the life of St. Christopher was given him as a subject he did not cry out against subjects in painting and talk about the absurdity of devotion and patriotism in art. He accepted the conditions and fulfilled them nobly. When Correggio was asked to paint an Assumption of the Madonna in the cupola of the Duomo at Parma he, too, accepted the conditions of subject and architectural surroundings and produced that wonderful circle of whirling angels which, seen from below, seems to rise higher and higher in the dome as though actually disappearing in the blue sky.

Hundreds of the Renaissance painters filled wall and altar spaces under similar limitations, producing Nativities, Flights into Egypt, Crucifixions, Resurrections, without ever a thought of quarrelling with their themes. They were hackneyed themes, too; but they knew that their success in the estimation of

XXX. – POUSSIN, Shepherds in Arcadia.   Louvre, Paris.

their fellow-craftsmen was largely dependent upon
the degree of freshness and originality with which
the subjects were treated. One of the astonishing
things about Tintoretto at Venice is that, coming at
the final day of the Renaissance, he should have handled the old time-worn and art-worn themes with
such novelty and power. The Annunciation, the
Nativity, the Flight, the Crucifixion in the Scuola
San Rocco at Venice are marvellous pieces of originality and invention. Before Tintoretto's time
there were innumerable " Marriages in Cana " painted for the Church, but that wonderful picture in the
Sacristy of the Salute at Venice goes beyond them
all (Plate 27). What was it to Titian or Moretto
that the early men had painted the " Assumption of
the Madonna " ? They did it over again with greater
originality and splendor.

Nor did the Renaissance painters wholly ignore
the audience for which their pictures were intended.
When Raphael painted the " Sistine Madonna " (Plate
28), he was most careful about the composition of
the group, about the drawing, the draperies, the
light, the color, the action of the figures. He studied
long and hard every decorative feature of the picture, that it might have grace of line and charm of
hue. Yes; and he also studied long and hard the
story it should tell to the congregation of the Black
Friars' Church at Piacenza, for whom the picture

was originally painted. It hung over the high altar of the church and was so conspicuously placed that the whole kneeling throng could see it. The curtains painted at the top of the picture are supposed to be the real altar-curtains, the ledge at the bottom where the cherubs rest is supposed to be the real altar-top. The angel-throng with the Madonna is coming down from heaven. She is walking on the clouds, coming forward to meet the kneeling worshippers and holding up to them the Child as the Hope of the World. Behind them is a great halo of light made up of angel-heads—the light of the Eternal Day. At the right St. Barbara kneeling turns away her face as though blinded by the radiance ; at the left San Sisto the martyr looks up to the Madonna and with one deprecating hand upon his bosom points outward with the other to the congregation as though saying : "Not for me, but for these poor souls in my keeping." It is impossible to ignore the story told in the picture ; impossible to say that it is an intrusion or should have been left out. There is nothing very decorative about the large round eyes of the Mother and Child—they were taken almost *verbatim* from the old Byzantine mosaics—but again it is impossible not to recognize the look of wonder they express and the specific meaning they must have had for the audience.

All of which would seem to suggest once more

that the theme in painting is at least not a hindrance, not a something to be got rid of, but a condition to be dealt with and handled illustratively in the same way that a given space of wall, panel or canvas is a condition to be dealt with decoratively. To say that painting shall reveal only " the appearance of things " and that the significance of those things shall count for naught is one extreme ; to say that objects shall depend solely upon their meaning and be regardless of decorative charm is the other extreme. Painters may choose either one or the other as becomes partisans (the great painters have always chosen both), but the spectator should cultivate a broader taste and exhibit a more discriminative mind. To Mr. Whistler, for instance, was given the sense of color, light, air, and the power to produce the glamour and the mystery of these in harmonies, symphonies, nocturnes—all of them decorative things lovely to look upon. Let us by all means admire them and love them ; but we should not allow ourselves to think that this alone is art, and all the products of the other men but so much rags and scrap-iron. Mr. Watts has a differently endowed mind. He grasps elemental truths of life and presents them in allegorical forms that are beautiful to think about, and Mr. Whistler does not like that. But never mind ; let us listen to Mr. Watts, too. He is a man of imagination, and what he has to say is well worth listening to, though he has not Mr. Whistler's point of view, and is somewhat lacking in the decorative quality.

Nor need we despise those painters whose equipment leads them to care as little for things decorative as for things symbolical. There are artistic minds that love to deal with facts as facts. Realism is healthful at least, and besides there may be much that is interesting in facts if we only study them long enough. Men like Courbet and Bonnat and Meissonier and Gérôme are not to be ignored. They are great students, great artists of their kind. Their minds move along scientific and archæological grooves, and in that respect they are quite different from the Whistlers, the Millets, and the Delacroixs; but I do not see why they are not entitled to admiration for what they do, especially when they do it so very well.

We should find something to admire in all of them, if we had more judgment and less prejudice. Unfortunately, we allow our likes to dictate to our taste. A certain form of art is agreeable to us, and therefore everything else is bad form and not art at all. Because one likes the Madonnas of Raphael is no reason for condemning the Madonnas of Holbein and Rubens. The landscape of Claude Lorraine is not incompatible with the landscape of Claude Monet. Both are good. But it is very difficult to make people see and believe that. Raising ourselves above prejudice is not easy of accomplishment. It is what is called, broadly, education—a difficult attainment to many, an absolute impossibility to some.

Indeed when we come to sum up these lectures we find their burden to be chiefly "Raising ourselves above prejudice." The special pleas of painters, whether for realization or decoration or illustration, are, of course, to be heard and accepted in part; but we are not to believe in any one of them to the utter exclusion of the others. Each is excellent of its kind, so far as it goes; but in our final judgment of the work of art we may conclude that the sum of the whole is greater than any of its parts, and that truth to nature, individuality, imagination, pictorial poetry, decorative beauty, subject—all the elements— go to the making of what is called "great art." Titian, Rubens, and Velasquez scorned none of these elements, advocated none of them exclusively; and you and I, who help make up the public, can perhaps do no better than base our principles of taste upon the works of those famed masters of the craft.

171D